D0177986

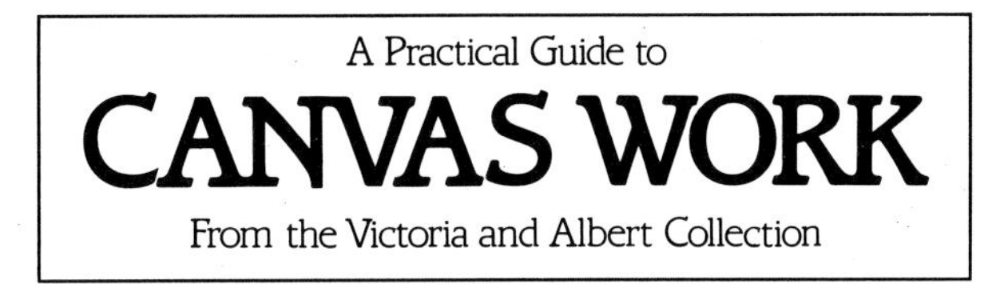
A Practical Guide to
CANVAS WORK
From the Victoria and Albert Collection

A Practical Guide to

CANVAS WORK

From the Victoria and Albert Collection

Introduction by Santina Levey
Edited by Linda Parry
Technical instructions by Valerie Jackson
Illustrations by Jil Shipley

UNWIN HYMAN
London Sydney

First published in Great Britain by Unwin Hyman, an imprint of Unwin Hyman Limited, 1987

UNWIN HYMAN LIMITED
Denmark House, 37–39 Queen Elizabeth Street, London SE1 2QB and
40 Museum Street, London WC1A 1LU

Allen & Unwin Australia Pty Ltd
8 Napier Street, North Sydney,
NSW 2060, Australia

Allen & Unwin New Zealand Ltd with the Port Nicholson Press, 60 Cambridge Terrace, Wellington, New Zealand

ISBN 0 04 440051 9

Cataloguing in Publication Data

Designed by Clare Clements
Filmset by MS Filmsetting Limited,
Frome, Somerset
Printed in Great Britain by
Blantyre Printing & Binding Co. Ltd,
London & Glasgow

ACKNOWLEDGEMENTS

The preparation of this book has involved the assistance and cooperation of the entire department of Textile Furnishings and Dress. Lynn Szygenda and Alyson Morris have both taken a special interest in the project and have done a great deal of backroom work. Debbie Sinfield has typed most of the text and Santina Levey and Natalie Rothstein have had the unenviable task of reading it and correcting inaccuracies. The photographs were taken by Philip de Bay and Daniel Magrath.

Valerie Jackson's detailed technical section and Jil Shipley's drawings have beautifully transformed this book into a working manual and we have all been sensitively nurtured by Elizabeth Brooke-Smith and Emma Callery of Unwin Hyman.

CONTENTS

FOREWORD

The purpose of this series of books is to introduce particular sections of the embroidery collection of the Victoria and Albert Museum and to serve as a bridge between the two quite separate historical and technical approaches to the subject. Patterns will be provided of selected Museum objects embroidered in many different styles and techniques and it is hoped that the additional technical information will inspire many readers to embroider items themselves, just as the experienced craftsperson should find inspiration from learning more of the history of the craft. Thus, by studying each embroidery technique separately through examples from the Museum's collection, a re-assessment of historic embroidery and its application to modern design will be possible.

INTRODUCTION

For practical reasons the selection of Museum examples for charting has been restricted to items showing small patterns, which are easily drawn and explained in a linear chart. It is hoped that the variations of repeating patterns and isolated motifs will suit most purposes and that these can be used either in restoration work, for the re-covering of an antique chair, for instance, or as inspiration for new patterns. In the items selected, only five different types of stitches (tent, cross, satin, Florentine and rococo) are represented whereas the Museum's collection of canvas embroidery provides a limitless fund of technical variations as is described in the following brief outline.

The Victoria and Albert Museum houses one of the World's largest embroidery collections and within it canvas work forms an important part of the European section. Such great medieval embroideries as the Syon Cope could perhaps be classed as canvas work since their linen grounds are entirely covered with embroidery, but the fineness of the work, the free-direction of some of the stitching and the extensive use of under-side couched metal thread, put them in a class apart. Closer to the modern idea of canvas work are the few coarser pieces which survive from the late 14th and 15th centuries. Those in the Museum's collection include the cushion cover in illus 1, which was embroidered in Westphalia in the early 15th century. Embroidered as it is with a variety of stitches, it shows that the technique was already fully developed.

The Museum's first sizeable group of canvas work pieces dates from the second half of the 16th and the first quarter of the 17th centuries. It consists mainly of furnishings and it reflects the role that textiles, including embroideries, then played in domestic interiors. Inventories of the day list innumerable canvas work wall hangings, table carpets, bed valances and cushion covers; all are represented in the collection. Among the earliest is the set of wall hangings known as the Oxburgh Hangings after the Norfolk manor house which has long been their home and where the three complete hangings are still displayed. The fourth, dismembered, hanging is at the Museum. In the centre of each complete hanging is a finely-worked panel (originally a cushion cover) which is decorated with emblematic motifs, ciphers and monograms relating to the lives of the two embroiderers who created them; Mary Queen of Scots and Elizabeth Countess of Shrewsbury (Bess of Hardwick). The central panel of the Cavendish Hanging (illus 3) is dated 1570 and it commemorates Bess of Hardwick's second husband, Sir William Cavendish. Arranged symmetrically round the central panel are a mixture of octagonal and cruciform panels worked with thick silk thread on a much coarser canvas. Many of these are also signed by the two noble amateurs who embroidered them. However the working of the padded frames in which they are set and the laying of the couched cord which decorates the green velvet ground to which they are applied, was undoubtedly done by a professional.

The Oxburgh Hangings illustrate the two basic ways in which canvaswork was used at that time – for solidly-embroidered complete panels and for appliqué. More common than the rather large applied panels of the Oxburgh Hangings were small, cut-out floral motifs known then as 'slips'. These have survived in quantity and must have been embroidered in their tens of hundreds in households throughout Britain. The pansy seen in the first charted canvas in this book is from a group of 12 slips. Another group in the Museum's collection has with it an original note dated 1596 and 1601 recording 79 slips in store in a chest (T.46 to 54–1972).

Although floral motifs seem to have been used most frequently for appliqué and were sewn down on woollen and velvet grounds for use in a full range of furnishings, animals and insects were also popular

Illus. 1: Cushion Cover. *The Virgin and Child with St Dorothy and angels. Linen embroidered with silk in plait, stem and herringbone stitches. Germany (Westphalia); early 15th century. 13in × 19in. (Museum no. 1324–1864)*

Illus. 2. Wall panel (detail). *Linen canvas embroidered with wool, silk, chenille and silver thread in tent, Hungarian, stem and satin stitch and couched work. French; early 18th century. Whole panel 9ft 10½in × 2ft 5¼in. (Museum no. T.390–1976)*

Illus. 3. The Cavendish hanging *from the set of four wall hangings known as the Oxburgh Hangings. Linen canvas embroidered with silk and silver-gilt thread in cross, tent and long-armed cross stitches, applied to green velvet decorated with couched cord. English; the central panel dated 1570. Other panels include initials ES and MR for Elizabeth, Countess of Shrewsbury and Mary Queen of Scots. 7ft $3\frac{1}{2}$in × 6ft 5in. (Museum no. T.30–1955)*

(*see* the 'spot' sampler and the embroidered panel on pages 30 and 34). Like the flowers, they reflect a general enthusiam for natural history and the origins of many of the embroidery patterns lay in the herbals and bestiaries printed during the 16th century. The motifs in these first three charts are somewhat removed from the original scholarly studies, but nearly all the monsters, fish, reptiles, animals, insects and birds that feature in the Oxburgh Hangings were copied directly from the second edition of Conrad Gesner's *Icones Animalium.* This serious scientific study was published in Zurich in 1560 and Mary Queen of Scots or, less likely, Bess of Hardwick, presumably owned a copy. Illustrations to a variety of printed books remained a fruitful source for embroidery designs throughout the late 16th, 17th and early 18th centuries.

The 1601 inventory of Hardwick Hall, built by Bess of Hardwick in the 1590s, still survives as do many of the embroideries mentioned in it. In addition to such items as 'an other long quition of grene velvett set with slips of nedleworke', there are references to solidly-embroidered panels like 'an other long quition of nedleworke, silke & Cruell of the storie of the Judgment of Saloman betwene the too women for the Childe' which can still be seen in the house. Unlike the applied work pieces and some of the other solidly-embroidered table carpets and valances, the Judgement of Solomon cushion was the work of a professional embroiderer. It belongs to a group of pictorial canvas work items produced in northern France or Flanders in the late 16th and early 17th centuries. Illus 4 shows a typical example from the Museum's collection. It is the centre piece of a wall hanging and although it illustrates a scene from classical literature, in this case *Lucretia's Banquet,* the figures are clothed in the elaborate dress worn at the French court around 1600. Some pictorial embroideries in a related style were worked in England but more typical of English professional work were rural scenes illustrating such pastimes as hawking and fishing against backgrounds containing mills and ponds, stately homes and rustic dwellings. The border of the Bradford table carpet is probably the most famous example of this style.

Elsewhere in Europe, of course, pictorial canvas work in a variety of distinctive national styles was being produced. Pictorial scenes were not the only motifs used to decorate large canvas work furnishings, and other popular designs included heraldic motifs, diapers, flowers and geometric patterns based on those of Turkish carpets, which were being imported into Europe in increasing quantity. Already popular in the late 16th century was the striking, vertical zig-zag pattern known now by various names including flame, Hungarian, Florentine and Bargello, but called then Irish stitch. It was a stitch of which there were many variations, some flamboyant and large-scale, others much more subdued with their effect depending as much on the use of colour as on the stitch itself, which was often simply a vertical tent stitch (*see* the charts taken from 18th century examples and the hand-screen on pages 40 and 48). It was to retain its popularity throughout the 17th and early 18th centuries and, in its large-scale form, its success was such that woven copies were manufactured in northern France.

Some of the canvas work furnishings of the 16th and 17th centuries were very large, with table carpets measuring up to 18 × 6 feet, but the technique was also used for small-scale items such as book covers, knife sheaths, shoes, pin cushions and purses. Many of these purses survive and they seem to have had a variety of uses, holding handkerchiefs, sewing tools or sweet-smelling herbs and powders which led to them being listed in the inventories as 'sweet bags'. They were decorated with floral motifs, often similar to those used for the appliqué slips, or with interlace and geometric patterns, which relate to those found on the spot-motif samplers of the day. These were initially the working tools of embroiderers, being samples of patterns and stitches that he or she wished to try-out or remember. The charted patterns from the German sampler, dated 1688 are of the spot-motif type but by this time the working of a sampler had become a more formalized part of a young woman's education.

The first motif charted from this sampler is worked in rococo stitch, particularly popular in the last quarter of the 17th and the first quarter of the 18th centuries. It can be found on small items like purses, pictures and work boxes but it was also used for large-scale pieces like the wall panel in illus. 5. This is one of six panels from a house in Hatton Garden, London and it

***Illus. 4. Centre panel** from a wall hanging: 'Lucretia's Banquet'. Canvas embroidered with wool and silk in tent stitch. French; about 1600. Whole: 9ft 9in × 5ft 6in. (Museum no. T.125–1913)*

***Illus. 5. Wall panel** from Hatton Garden, London. Canvas embroidered with wool in tent, brick, cross, crosslet and rococo stitches, with couched work and French knots. English; Late 17th century. 7ft 8in × 3ft 10in. (Museum no. 518–1896)*

illustrates a number of ways in which the use of canvas work was changing. Although free-hanging wall coverings continued to be worked, mainly by amateurs, almost until the middle of the 18th century, their more common form in the late 17th century was as canvas work panels stretched on frames and fitted to the wall, usually within a wooden surround. Less commonly, they were mounted edge to edge almost in the manner of wallpaper, which was beginning to be used as an alternative to the woven silks with which walls were also covered at this time. Stretched canvaswork panels also began to be used for free-standing screens and, during the 18th century, for smaller fire-screens, pole-screens and hand-screens (*see* page 48).

By the late 17th century, table carpets had gone out of use in the majority of households, whose owners now wanted to display table tops of fine wood, often intricately inlaid. They were replaced however by floor carpets, which were growing in use and which were to be embroidered by professionals and amateurs throughout the 18th and 19th centuries. Similarly, as upholstered funiture came increasingly into use during the second half of the 17th century, embroidered cushions were replaced by canvas work chair seats, backs and entire covers (See furnishing fabrics on pages 40–47).

Stylistically, the Hatton Garden hanging in illus 5 is very different from the English embroideries of the early 17th century. The rather solid, classical columns with which it is decorated have foliated capitals reflecting the Baroque style, which is also expressed in the exuberant foliage. This relates to the designs of the crewelwork curtains which were being worked in England at this time. They illustrate the fruitful exchange of ideas which took place between East and West at the turn of the 17th and 18th centuries and exotic Eastern birds are often found amongst the Baroque foliage. The Hatton Garden panels however are more insular, and their birds and animals look backwards to English designs of the early 17th century.

Considerably more up-to-date is a set of French wall panels which the Museum acquired in 1976 (illus 2). Although only slightly later in date than the Hatton Garden panels, they are strikingly different. The variety of motifs of which they are composed include bizarre forms and foliage taken from contemporary French woven silks, blue and white Chinese porcelain, garden statues and urns in the style of those used to ornament the gardens at Versailles and figures based on the paintings and tapestry designs of David Teniers the Younger. Both these French panels and those from Hatton Garden employ a variety of stitches but the French pieces are grounded with silver thread couched in spirals. This is a technique found in a number of French professional canvas embroideries of the late 17th and early 18th centuries, including a set of hangings showing Louis XIV (1638–1715) in allegorical representations of *The Elements*. The Museum possesses one hanging showing Louis XIV as Jupiter (T.106–1978) in the element of *Air*, but in this case the ground is worked with wool in tent stitch.

Even allowing for the difference in size of the various furnishings, the greatest quantity of canvas used in the 18th century was undoubtedly employed in working fitted chair seats and backs. Many were embroidered professionally but a huge quantity was produced by amateurs. Designs ready-drawn on the relatively closely-woven canvas grounds could be bought from the needlework repositories and, in some instances, the finer details, such as the faces, were pre-worked over single threads. The larger stitches used for the remainder of the panel were worked over pairs of threads, which were pulled together so that the worked canvas resembled the Penelope canvas of the 19th century. It is also clear that the more skilful embroideresses drew out their own designs, in many instances making use of printed sources. The chair seat charted on page 52 makes use of a single flower in a repeating pattern but naturalistic flowers arranged in bunches or displayed in baskets were probably more common and, during the 1730s and 1740s, they were also used to form bold and decorative borders to pictorial centre pieces. Illus 6 shows such a border, on a typical deep yellow ground, in use on a sofa. This is part of a set of sofa and six chairs decorated with scenes based on William Kent's illustrations for John Gay's *Fables* (1727). The floral borders were probably pre-drawn on the canvas and the central scenes, which are not so competently drawn out, were possibly the work of the embroideress. The fact that amateur

Illus 6. Sofa seat (right hand side). *Jugglers from William Kent's illustrations of John Gay's Fables, first published in 1727. Canvas embroidered with wool and silk in cross and tent stitch. English; 1730s. Whole width 54⅝in × 20⅝in. (Museum no. T.473–1970)*

Illus 7. Chair seat: Summer. *Designed by Alan Walton and embroidered by Lady Glyn. Canvas embroidered with wool in cross, tent and byzantine stitch. One of a set representing the seasons. English; about 1938. Length approx 16¼in × 20½in. (Museum no. T.1–1959)*

embroidery, sometimes worked to amateur designs, was used on furniture of the highest quality is illustrated in the account books of Thomas Chippendale. In the mid-1760s, for example, he supplied Sir Edward Knatchbull with '8 French chairs with rosewood feet, the backs and seats covered with your own needlework'.

Sets of 24 or 48 chair seats and backs could take several years to complete and, perhaps because they were not ready before the fashion for decorated upholstery gave way to simpler styles during the 1770s, many were never used. The Museum possesses one collection of 20 pictorial chair seats (T.120 to S–1956) which have never been stretched and mounted.

Although carpets continued to be embroidered until the very end of the 18th century, there was no place for decorative canvas work in the plain neo-classical interiors of the day. Most embroiderers turned to silk embroidery and to tambour work. Those who retained a love for wool and canvas produced needle-painted copies of paintings in irregular long and short stitches that ignored the underlying woven grid.

The opening years of the 19th century therefore saw the popularity of canvas work at a low ebb, although this was shortly to be changed by the introduction of the technique known as Berlin woolwork. It was in 1804 that a Berlin publisher produced embroidery patterns printed on a graph paper, so that they could be copied square by square on to a square-meshed canvas. The earliest patterns were hand-painted and the delicate floral designs were intended to be worked with an extensive range of coloured wools on a fine canvas. The wools used were zephyr merino wools from Saxony, dyed in Berlin with a huge variety of clear, glowing colours. The sale of Berlin patterns and wools gradually spread outside Germany and began to increase dramatically as more Romantic styles developed in the late 1810s and 1820s. By the 1830s, patterns and wools were manufactured in England, France and other countries, although the original name remained. The original floral patterns were joined by pictorial designs of varying quality, some of which were exceedingly ambitious. At the 1851 Exhibition, for example, six versions of Leonardo da Vinci's 'The Last Supper' were shown, as well as copies of paintings by Landseer and other 19th-century artists. Although the technique could be used imaginatively and an increasing range of stitches and patterns was employed by the more skilled embroiderers, the third quarter of the 19th century saw the technique decline in quality. Increasingly coarse double canvas, called 'Penelope', almost entirely replaced the finer single-thread canvases. It was machine-woven in cotton and gave a much stiffer texture to the embroidery and a harder edge to the finished design. Thicker wools were also used and the glowing Berlin colours were replaced by harsh aniline dyes, many of which turned an ugly muddy colour with time.

It was in reaction to the strangle-hold of Berlin woolwork that William Morris and the other innovators of the later 19th century turned away from canvas work to such techniques as crewelwork and appliqué. During the first half of the 20th century, the more adventurous embroiderers concentrated on varieties in surface texture and stitches, effects not readily available with canvas work. Small but significant artistic groups such as the Omega Workshop did use the technique to show off their exciting original designs, however, and fashionable interior designers of the 1920s and 1930s used canvas embroidery as part of their revivalist interiors. Skilled amateurs were often responsible for the execution of these flat designs and examples in the Museum by Duncan Grant and Alan Walton (illus 7) show how the technique was adapted for highly original purposes.

An interest in European peasant embroidery techniques from the 1920s onwards saw a revival of interest in counted thread embroidery, usually worked in cross stitch, but on closer-woven grounds rather than canvas. The exhibitions and publications organized by both the Embroiderers' Guild and the Needlework Development Scheme promoted variations on the technique, including the use of canvas grounds, which re-appeared in the repertoire of most 20th-century embroiderers, both amateur and professional.

A renewed interest in canvas embroidery has developed since the 1960s and a number of artists and designers have turned to the technique to provide the clarity of design and variety of colour that their work demands. Leading commercial designers in the field, such as Lillian Delevoryas and Kaffe Fassett, supply numerous original designs to commercial manufacturers to be made into kits for making up at home and with renewed exciting uses the technique has once again achieved a respectability and popularity not known since the middle of the 19th century.

Because of refurbishment programmes and financial restraints, galleries in the Victoria and Albert Museum are subject to closure from time to time but, because of the great variety of periods and nationalities represented in the canvas work collection it is likely that some examples will always be available.

The Textile Materials and Technique Galleries contain a large number of examples of canvas work arranged chronologically by country: Britain and Europe (Rooms 100 and 101), The Near East (Room 99), The Far East (Room 98). and European peasant embroidery (Room 96). Because canvas embroidery has been worked almost continually since Medieval times, examples can also be found in most of the main Art and Design Galleries of the Museum, which show mixed displays of objects from the same period. Visitors interested in the technique should visit the Medieval Treasury (Gallery 43), The English Renaissance Gallery (Rooms 52–54) and displays covering the late 17th to 20th centuries (Rooms 118–125 and Room 74). Continental examples are displayed in Galleries 1 to 7.

TECHNICAL INSTRUCTIONS ON GENERAL CANVAS WORK

The craft of canvas work is sometimes wrongly referred to as tapestry, but the techniques, in fact, bear no resemblance to each other. Tapestry is woven, whereas in canvas work open grid fabric is filled with individually-sewn stitches of various kinds.

Many modern canvas workers are very adventurous in the stitches they use to embellish their canvas but the designs from the Victoria and Albert Museum featured in this book only use five basic stitches—tent, cross, satin, Florentine and rococo—all of which should be easy to master quite quickly with the help of the diagrams.

Close stitching on an already strong background forms a very firm textured fabric which can be used for cushions, upholstery or on a large scale, for rugs.

WHAT YOU NEED FOR CANVAS WORK

Canvas

Most canvas is made of linen or cotton, though some modern ones are also made of synthetics. They come in different gauges and the gauge chosen must be suitable for the intended project. For example, only a simple design with blocks of colour can be achieved on a large-gauge canvas, while a delicate, detailed design will need a small-gauge canvas.

To find the gauge of a canvas, place a ruler along a thread and count the number of meshes (points at which the threads intersect) to the inch. Don't count the holes.

There are two main types of canvas, single thread and double thread. The advantage of single thread is that you can use it for any stitch. Double thread canvas, which is measured by the number of *pairs* of threads per inch, enables you to work stitches of different sizes on the same canvas when the double threads are separated. The size of double thread canvas is indicated by two numbers separated by a line (eg 10/20), the smaller number means the number of double intersections per inch and the larger means the number of single intersections when the threads are separated.

Single thread canvas ranges from about 32 to 10 threads per inch and double from about 3 (rug size) to 14, or even finer. Canvas comes in colours that vary from brown to cream to white.

Most of the earlier designs in this book were worked on fine canvas and details of these early grounds are found in the introduction.

Threads

There are many different threads to choose from for canvas work. The choice will depend on the gauge of the canvas and the stitch – the larger the gauge, the heavier the thread must be.

Wool is very hardwearing and you can choose from tapestry wool, which is a thick, single strand wool; crewel wool, a finer single strand wool; or Persian, a three strand wool, the strands of which can be separated and used singly.

Knitting wool is not usually recommended for canvas work, as it breaks easily due to its short fibres.

In addition to wool, there are embroidery cottons in different finishes and stranded silks and rayons.

All these threads come in a wide variety of lovely colours, so you should have no difficulty in finding those to match the designs in this book.

Needles

Tapestry needles with large eyes and blunt ends are used for canvaswork, as needles with sharp points will split the threads.

Too small a needle for the canvas will cause the thread to wear at the eye of the needle as it is dragged through the canvas. Too large a needle will distort the threads already in place.

Tapestry needles range in size from 14 to 26 (the larger the number, the smaller the needle).

As a rough guide, a 14 to 18 needle can be used on a 10 to 12 gauge canvas, a 26 needle on a 32 to 22 gauge canvas.

Scissors

Dressmaker's scissors are useful for cutting canvas and a sharp, pointed pair of embroidery scissors will be needed for cutting threads and for unpicking.

You will also need a thimble and a tape measure.

Frames

A sewing frame gives a better result than working in the hand. It prevents the work distorting and by keeping the tension of the canvas even, it allows for more even stitching.

In a square or 'slate' frame, the canvas is attached to the frame at the sides with tapes and the top and bottom ends are rolled round rollers. The frame will hold any length of canvas as long as it is no wider than the tape on the rollers. A slate frame on a stand leaves your hands free to work the canvas.

Smaller, hoop frames are best for fine canvases and small pieces of work.

Home-made stretcher frames can be made from a picture frame or from four pieces of wood nailed together. The canvas can either be drawing-pinned to the frame or taped, as on a slate frame.

STARTING WORK

After being pulled through the canvas repeatedly, threads wear thin, so a working thread should only be about 20in long at the most.

Try a few stitches on the canvas before work, to see if you have the right thickness of thread. Each stitch should look plump, not bald and skimpy.

To start, tie a knot in the end of the thread and take the needle through the canvas from the right side, a few stitches from the beginning of the new row. Stitch along the row, catching the long thread at the back as you go. When you reach the knot, snip it off.

To fasten off, weave the thread through the underside of the stitches and snip the end off.

Try not to start any end threads in line with each other or a ridge will form.

As you stitch, keep up an even tension, neither pulling the wool too tight nor leaving loops on the surface.

When stitching, you can take the stitch from front to back and through to the front again as in ordinary sewing, but if working on a frame, use stab stitching – stab the needle from front to back and then from back to front.

When working in the hand, start at the centre and work outwards, so that the work does not have to be crumpled up in your hand.

To make for a smoother surface, try to plan the rows of stitches so that the needle comes up in an empty hole and goes down in a full one.

If the thread twists while sewing, allow the needle and thread to dangle, then they will untwist and you can continue sewing without forming knots.

CHARTS

On a chart, the vertical and horizontal lines of the graph paper correspond to the threads of the canvas.

The charts in this book are box charts, so the squares on the graph paper represent the threads and intersections of the canvas. When using tent stitch, therefore, one square equals one intersection. With straight stitches, one square indicates one thread or intersection of the total length of the stitch.

A chart may be a whole design or it may be a part of a repeating design. When using a whole design chart, the canvas used will have the same number of threads as the number of lines on the chart and the gauge of the canvas used will decide the size of the finished work.

If you intend to enlarge a design, experiment with larger gauge canvas and thicker thread to find out how small motifs will look on a larger scale – some may not translate as readily as others. A large design can be reduced, with finer detail added, for finer canvas.

Since there is no point in charting the same motif over and over again, partial designs are used to chart repeating patterns, as in Florentine work, for example, when a motif or row is charted.

Symmetrical designs are often charted in half or quarter charts. The repeats meet and are reversed at the centre of the design. Such charts are not difficult to follow as long as the centre of the canvas is clearly marked out.

Canvas frays, so always add two inches all round and bind the edges with tape.

Label the top of the canvas and mark the centre with horizontal and vertical lines.

In this book, symbols indicate colours in the charts.

ESTIMATING THREAD QUANTITIES

The amount of thread needed will depend on the type of stitch and the gauge of the canvas, so to find out how much thread you will need, work a square inch in the chosen stitch, thread and canvas. Work with 20in lengths, find out how many you used per square inch and multiply the length by the number. It is then a fairly easy matter to work out how many inches of that stitch and colour are to be used over the whole area. To be on the safe side, allow an extra small percentage for each colour.

FINISHING

Most canvas work becomes distorted during the working, especially when diagonal stitches are used. To bring the work back to its square shape, it should be steam pressed, face down under a damp cloth, then pinned to a board face upwards with all edges square and straight and allowed to dry.

STITCHES

Tent stitch

This stitch can be done horizontally, vertically or diagonally. It covers the ground quickly and can be used with padding or 'tramming', to make a thicker texture.

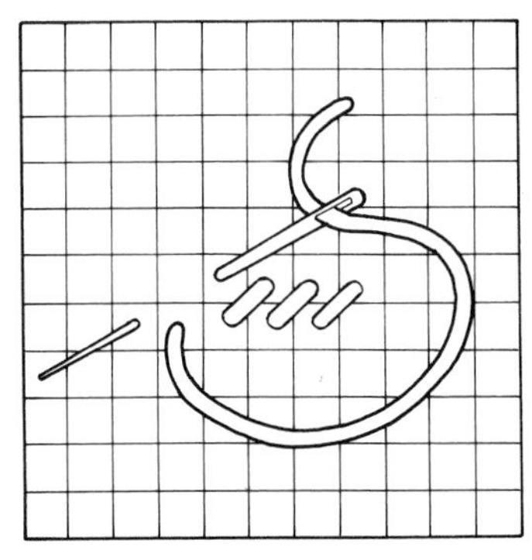

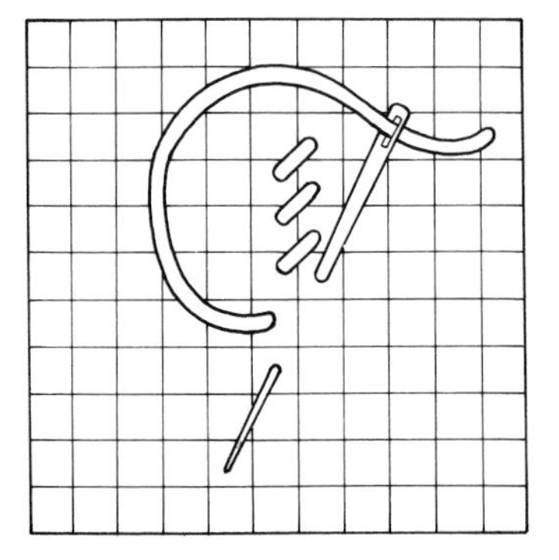

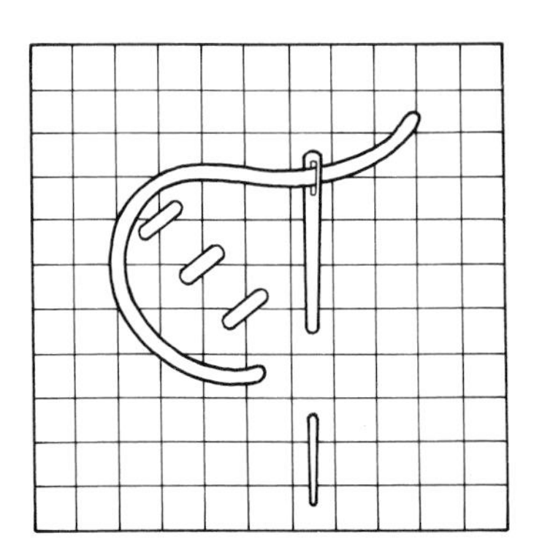

Cross stitch
A hardwearing stitch which is useful for backgrounds and for geometric designs.

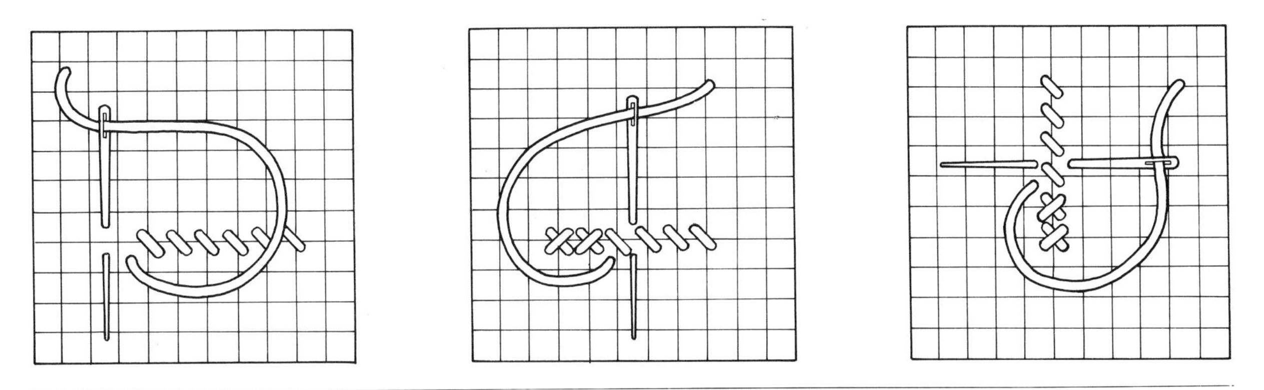

Satin stitch
The width of the rows can be varied, as can the number of stitches in the row. The rows slant in opposite directions.

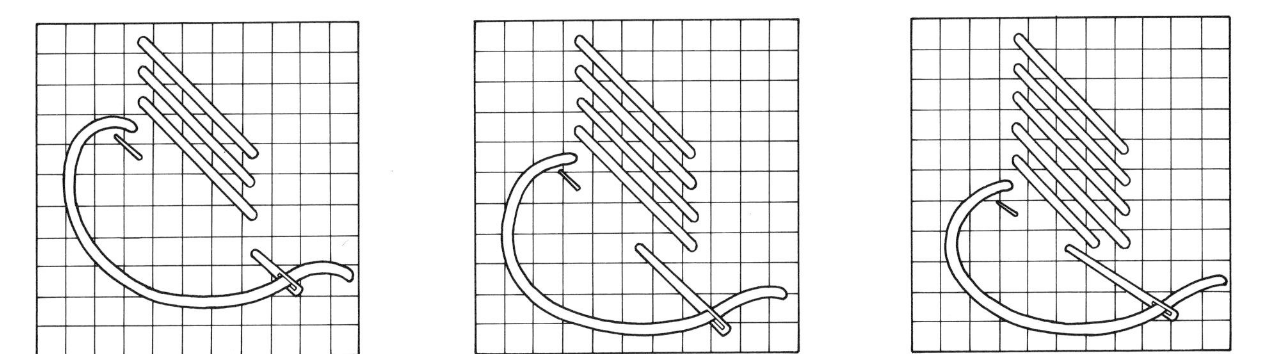

Florentine
Florentine work is made in straight stepped stitches, each differently-coloured row placed next to the other to form a zig-zag pattern up and down the canvas. The stitches can be long or short or a mixture of both. Here they are shown stitched over four threads, which is shown on the charts as four squares.

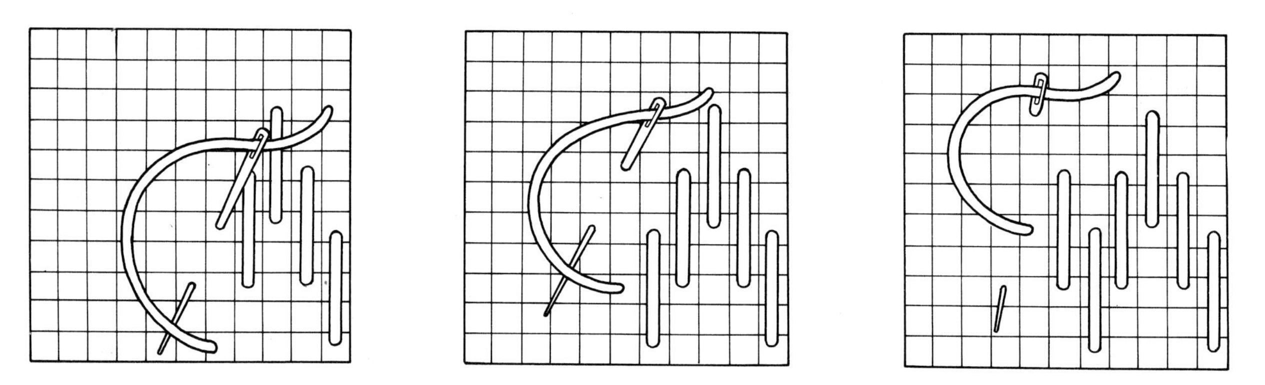

Rococo
Long straight stitches are held down by short straight stitches, the long stitches becoming bowed in the process. A small hole appears at the junction of the four completed stitches, giving an attractive texture to the work.

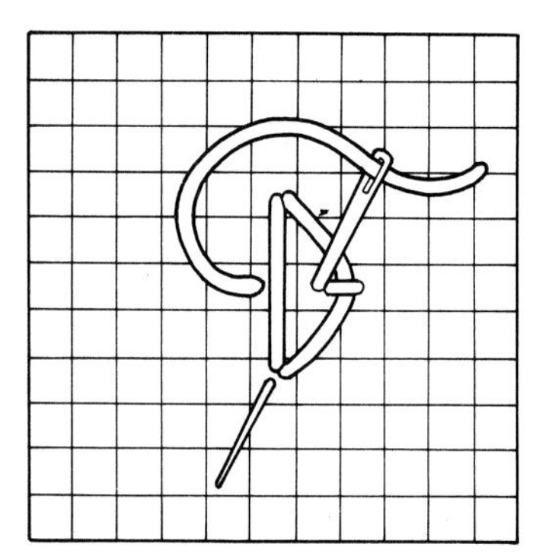

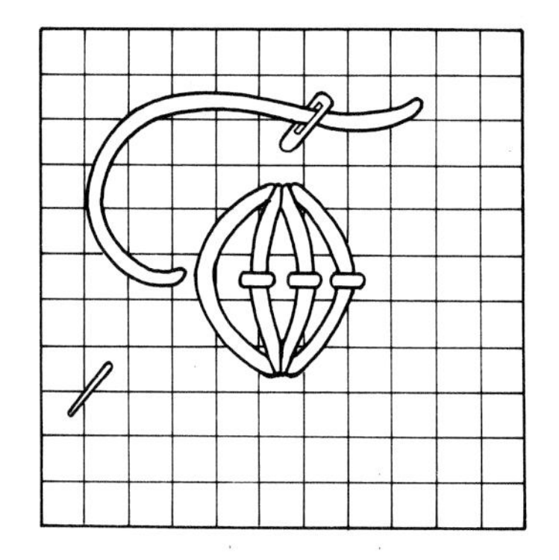

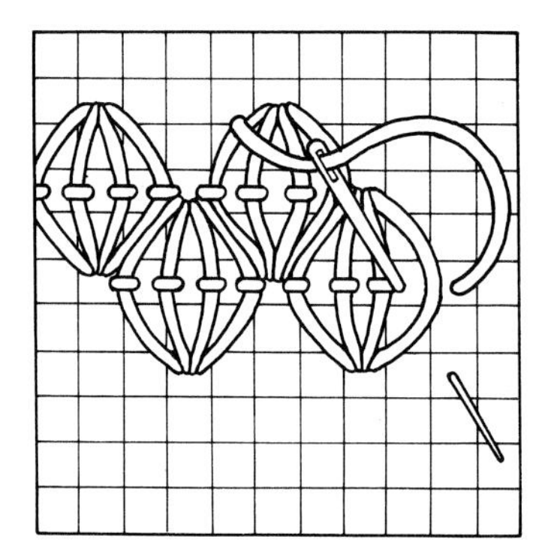

Rococo stitch: 4 squares = 1 stitch

yellow ⊡

pink ⧄

points at which 10 threads go into one hole (see smallest diagram opposite) ■

See German 17th century sampler on page 36.

EMBROIDERED SLIP

See photograph on page 28
Linen canvas embroidered with silk in tent stitch.
ENGLISH, about 1600
Height (approx) 8in × $7\frac{3}{4}$in
Detail charted $1\frac{3}{4}$in × $1\frac{5}{8}$in
Museum no. Circ. 748B–1925

Key for chart opposite

Tent stitch: 1 square = 1 stitch

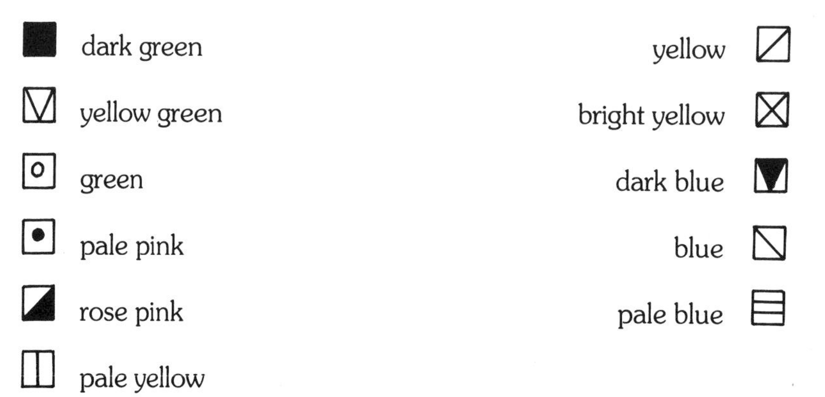

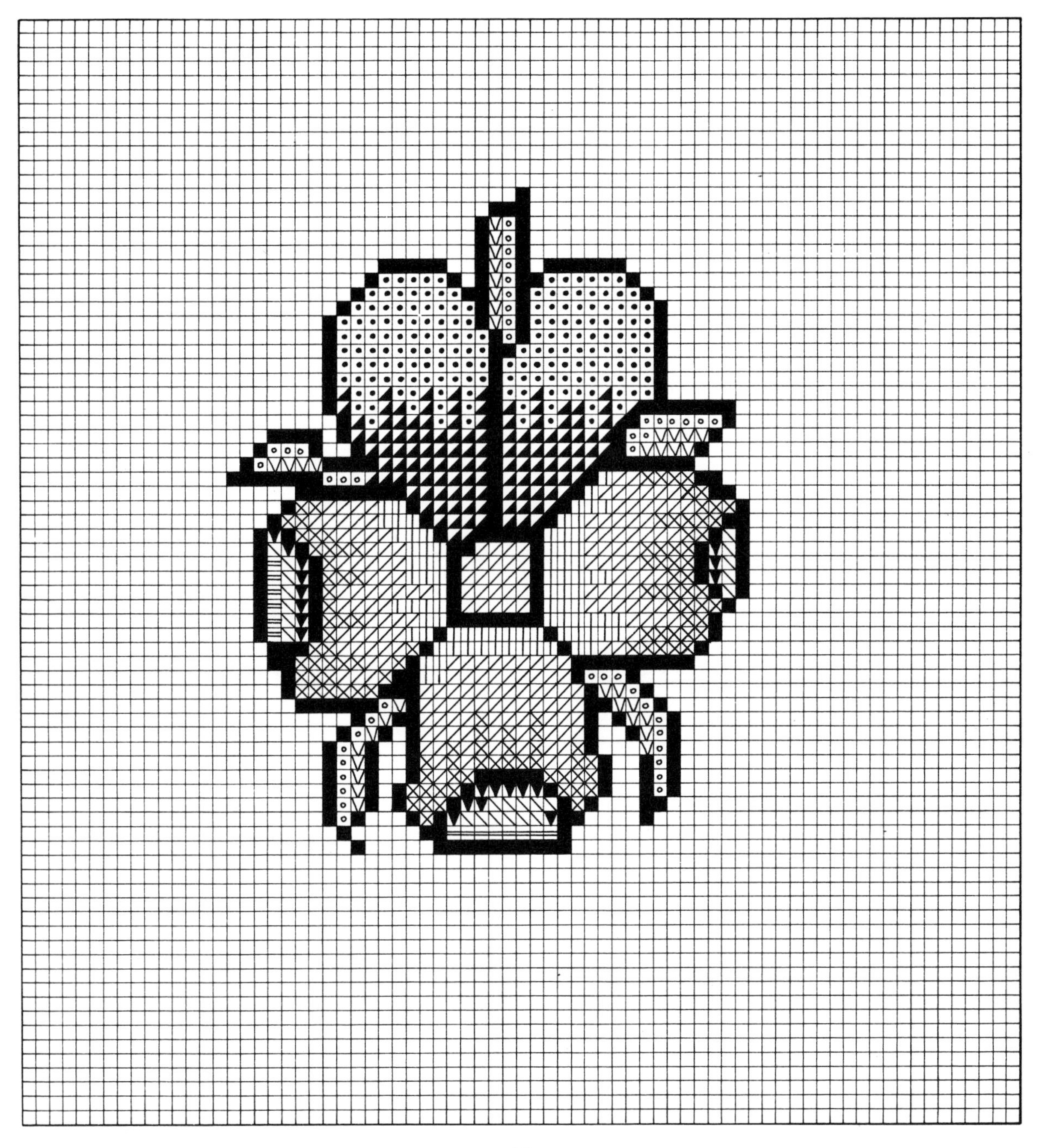

Embroidered slip (chart page 27)

Spot-motif sampler (chart page 31)

A SPOT-MOTIF SAMPLER

See photograph on page 29

Linen canvas embroidered with silver and silk embroidery in buttonhole, chain, stem and tent stitch, the latter worked in two directions. The metal flower stems are worked in plaited stitch.

ENGLISH, early 17th century. The panel is signed 'E.B.' in the lower left hand corner.

Section shown $8\frac{3}{4} \times 9\frac{1}{2}$in (worked in tent stitch)

Detail charted $1\frac{1}{2} \times 1\frac{1}{4}$in

Museum no. 282–1894

Key for chart opposite

Tent stitch: 1 square = 1 stitch

brown

mid-blue

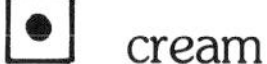

cream

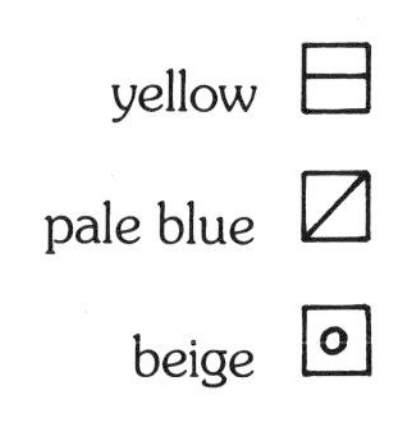

yellow

pale blue

beige

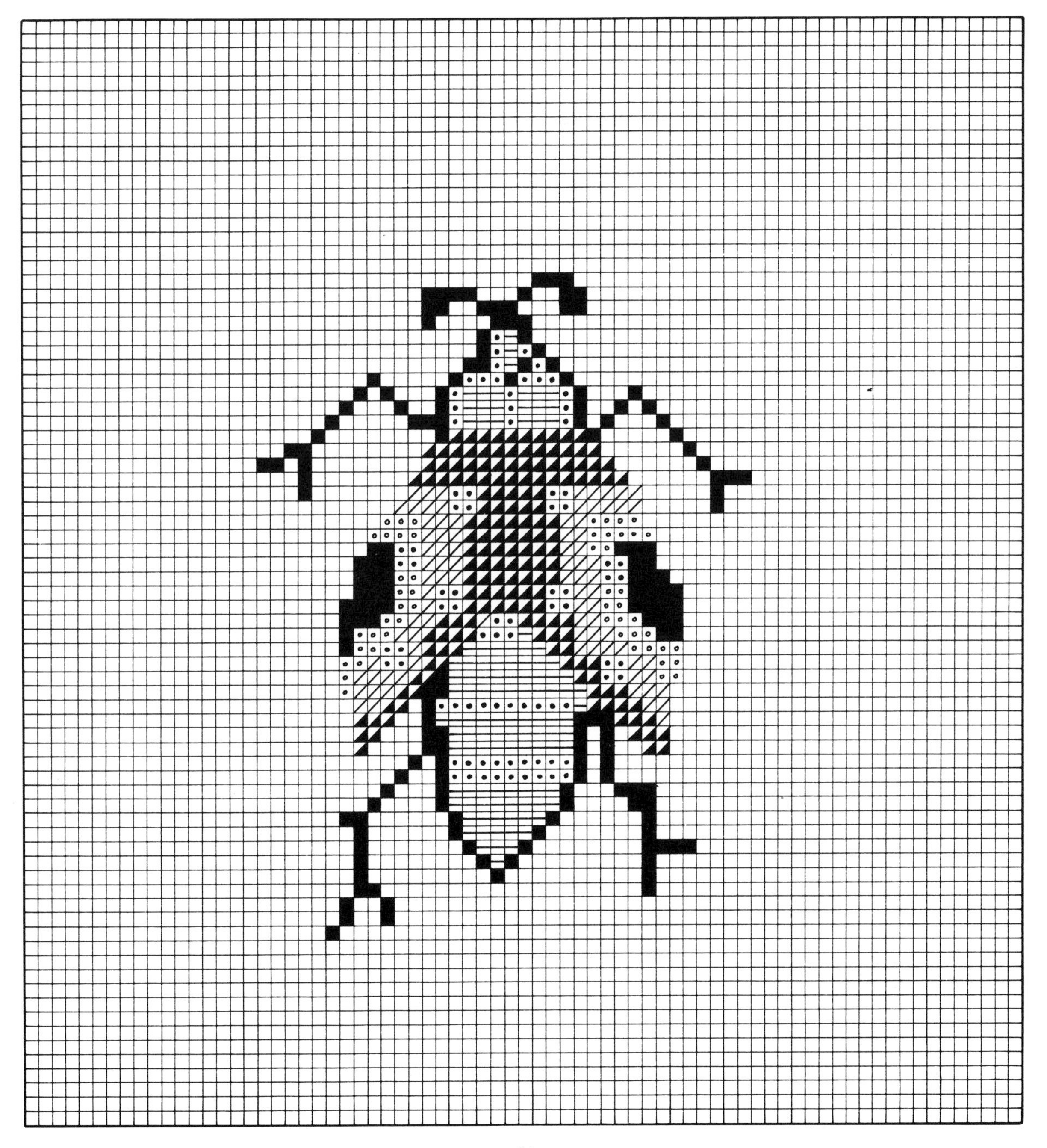

FRAGMENT OF AN EMBROIDERED PANEL

Linen canvas embroidered with silks and gold and silver thread mostly in tent stitch. The metal flower stems are couched to the ground in silk with rosettes of twisted metal purl. The embroidered ground has been worked in concentric squares of cream silk which shows clearly on the back of the panel.
ENGLISH, early 17th century
6½in × 8¼in
Detail charted 1¾in × 1in (worked in tent stitch)
Given by Miss Mary Davies
Museum no. T.221–1931

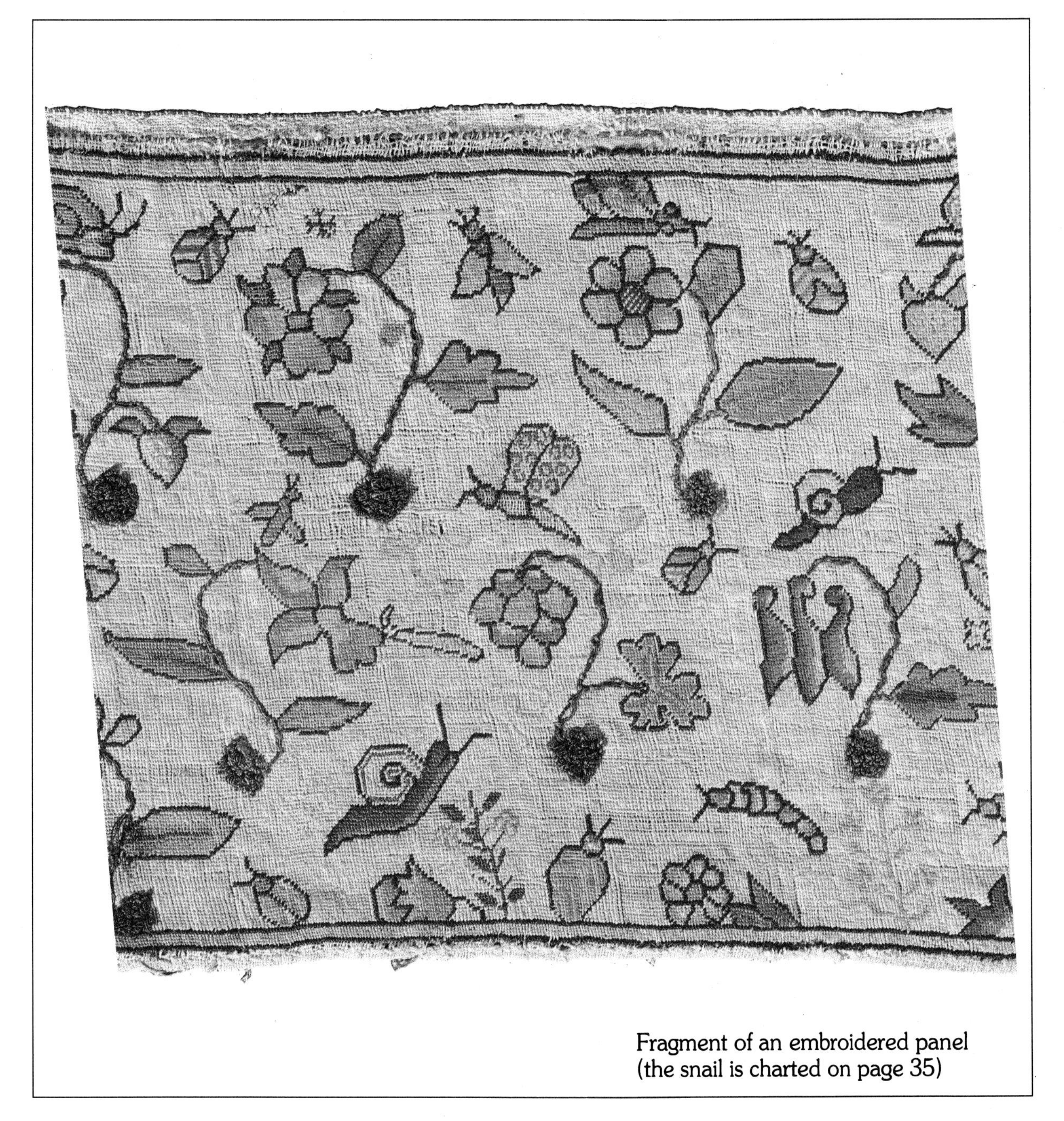

Fragment of an embroidered panel
(the snail is charted on page 35)

Key for chart opposite

Tent stitch: 1 square = 1 stitch

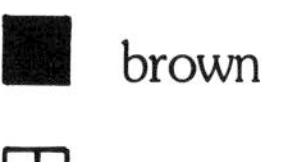

brown

light brown

beige

blue

cream

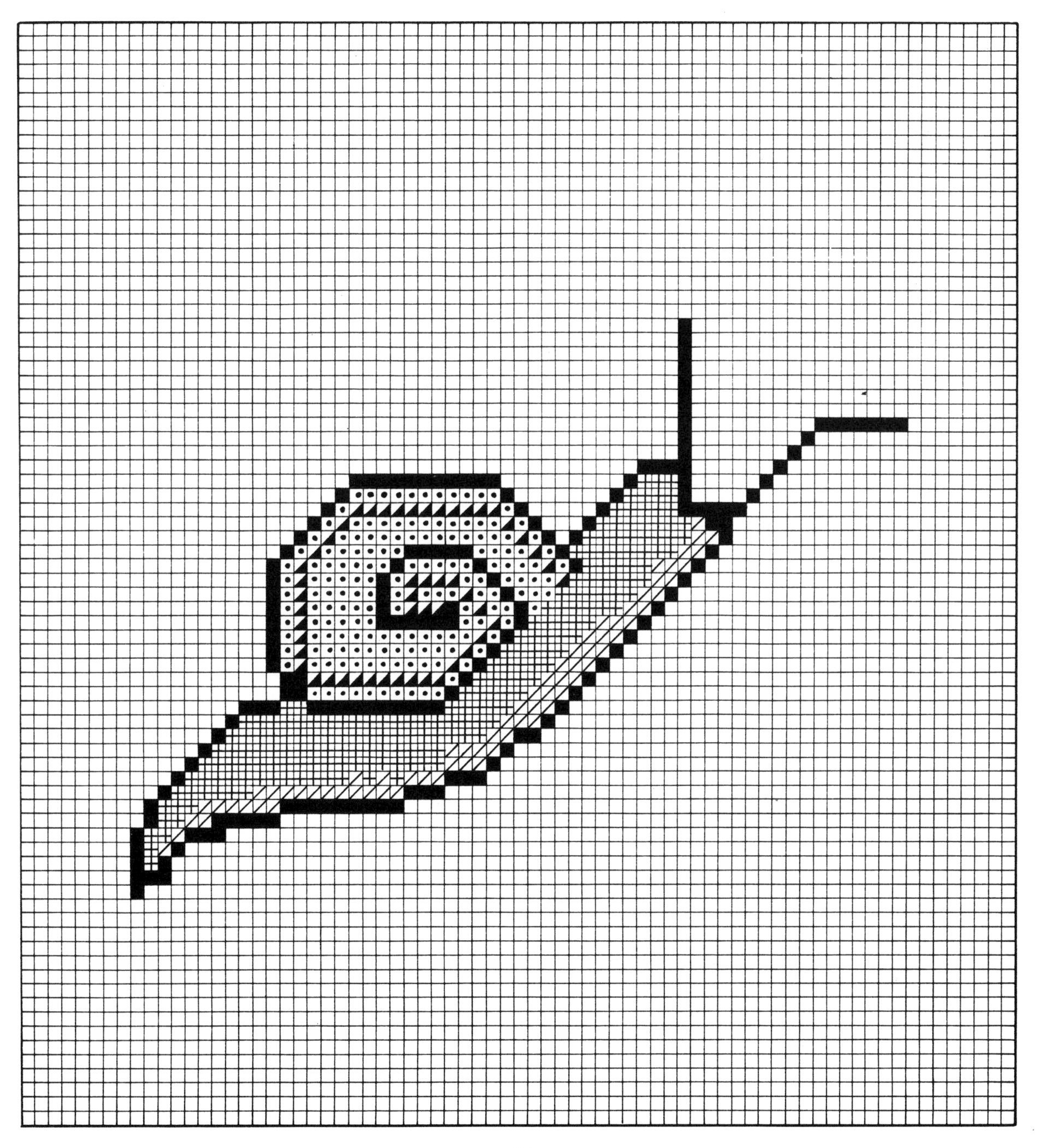

GERMAN 17TH-CENTURY SAMPLER

Linen canvas embroidered with silk in tent, cross, satin, eye, rice and rococo stitch.
GERMAN, dated 1688 and initialled 'D.M.W.'.
Whole sampler 23in × 9in
Detail as in illustration approx. $8\frac{3}{4} \times 9$in
Museum no. 104–1880

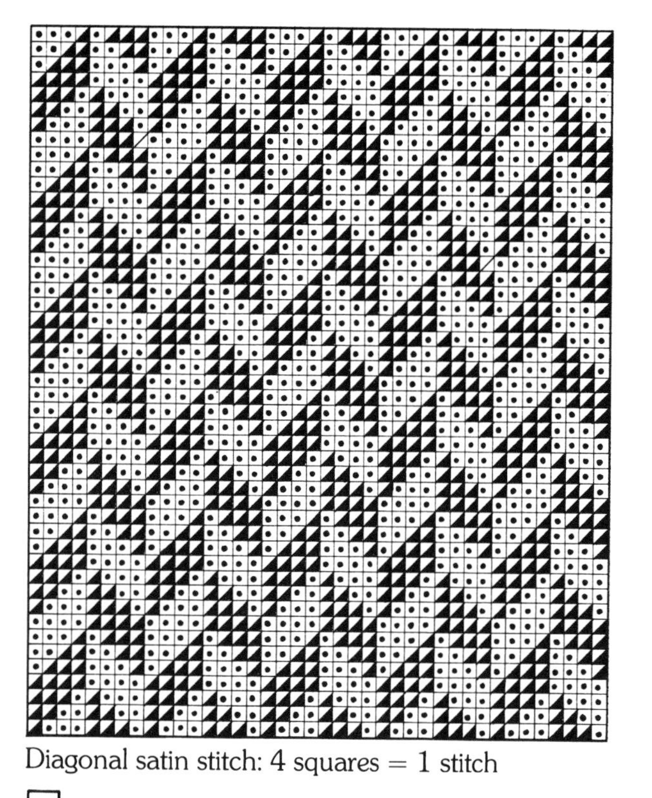

Diagonal satin stitch: 4 squares = 1 stitch

- yellow
- grey

For Rococo stitch chart see page 25

Key to chart opposite

Tent stitch: 1 square = 1 stitch

- cream
- pale pink
- pink
- rusty pink
- yellow
- gold
- mauve
- mid-blue
- pale blue
- black

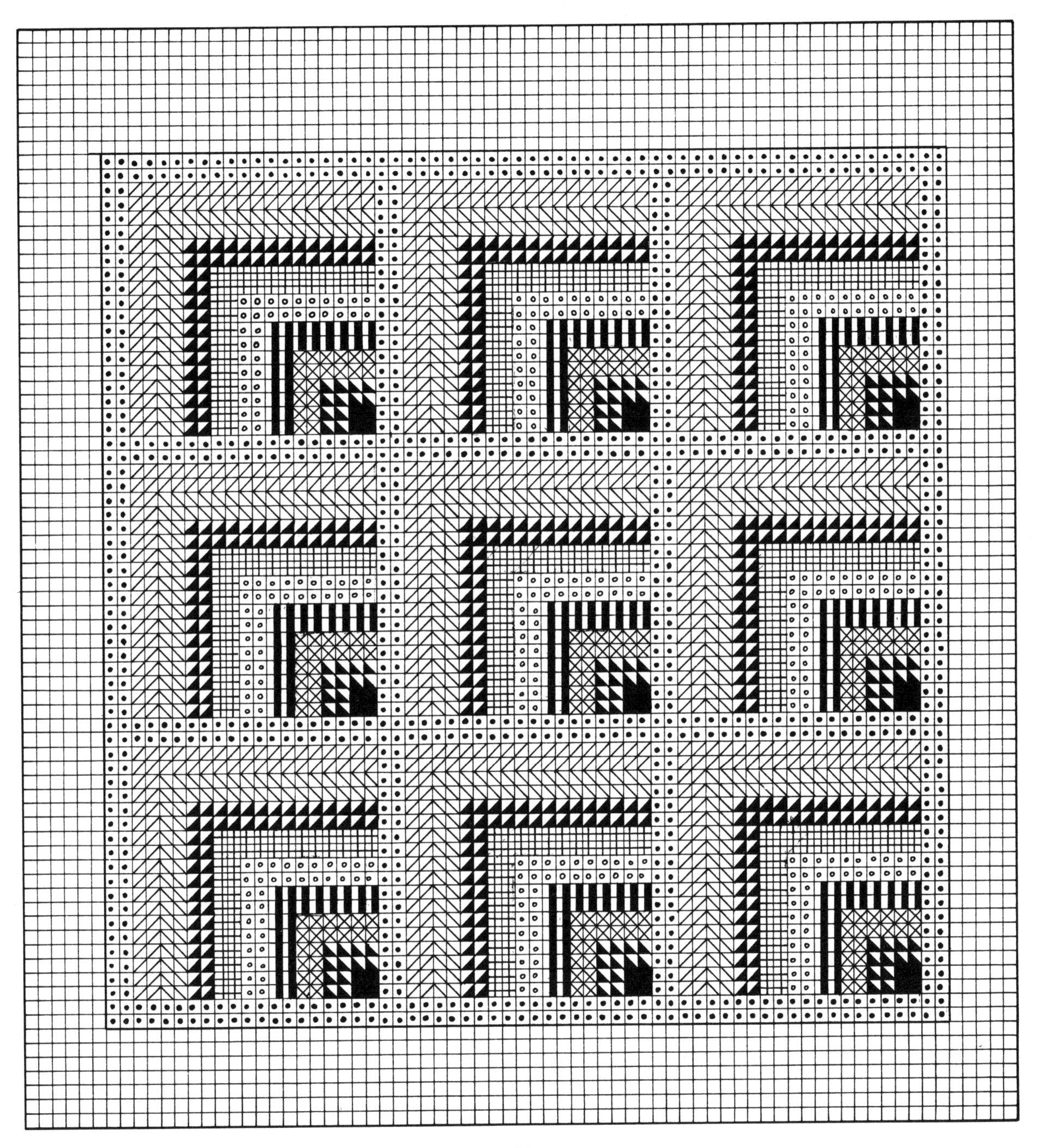

TWO ITALIAN UPHOLSTERY FABRICS

See photographs on facing page and pages 44–45
Linen canvas embroidered with silks in Florentine stitch.
ITALIAN, early 18th century
A. $10\frac{1}{4}$in × $5\frac{1}{4}$in
Pattern repeat: (shell motif) $3\frac{1}{2}$in × $2\frac{3}{4}$in
Museum nos. 755, 756–1894
B. $7\frac{1}{4}$in × $9\frac{1}{8}$in
Pattern repeat: (2 motifs) $5\frac{1}{2}$in × $4\frac{3}{4}$in

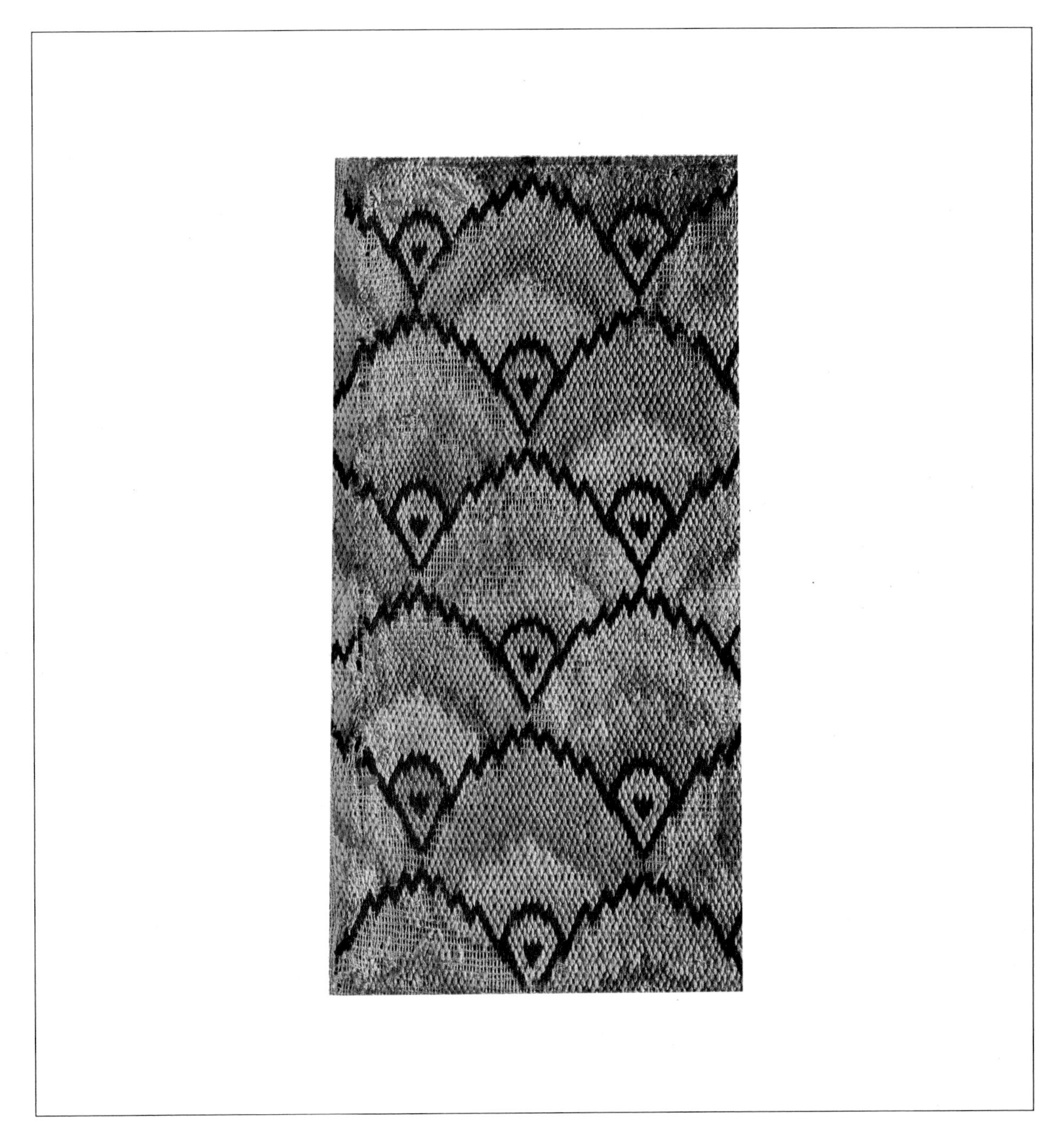

Key to chart opposite

Florentine stitch: 4 squares = 1 stitch

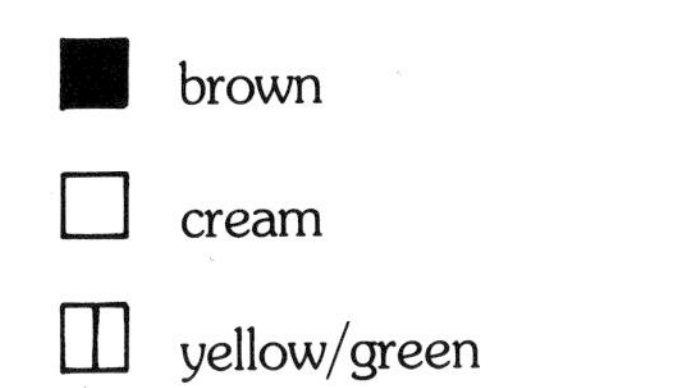

Key to chart on pages 46–47

Florentine stitch: 4 squares = 1 stitch

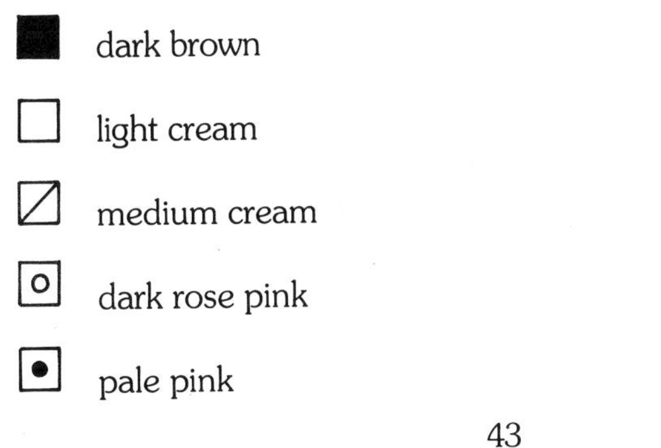

18th-century Italian upholstery fabric (charts pages 46–47)

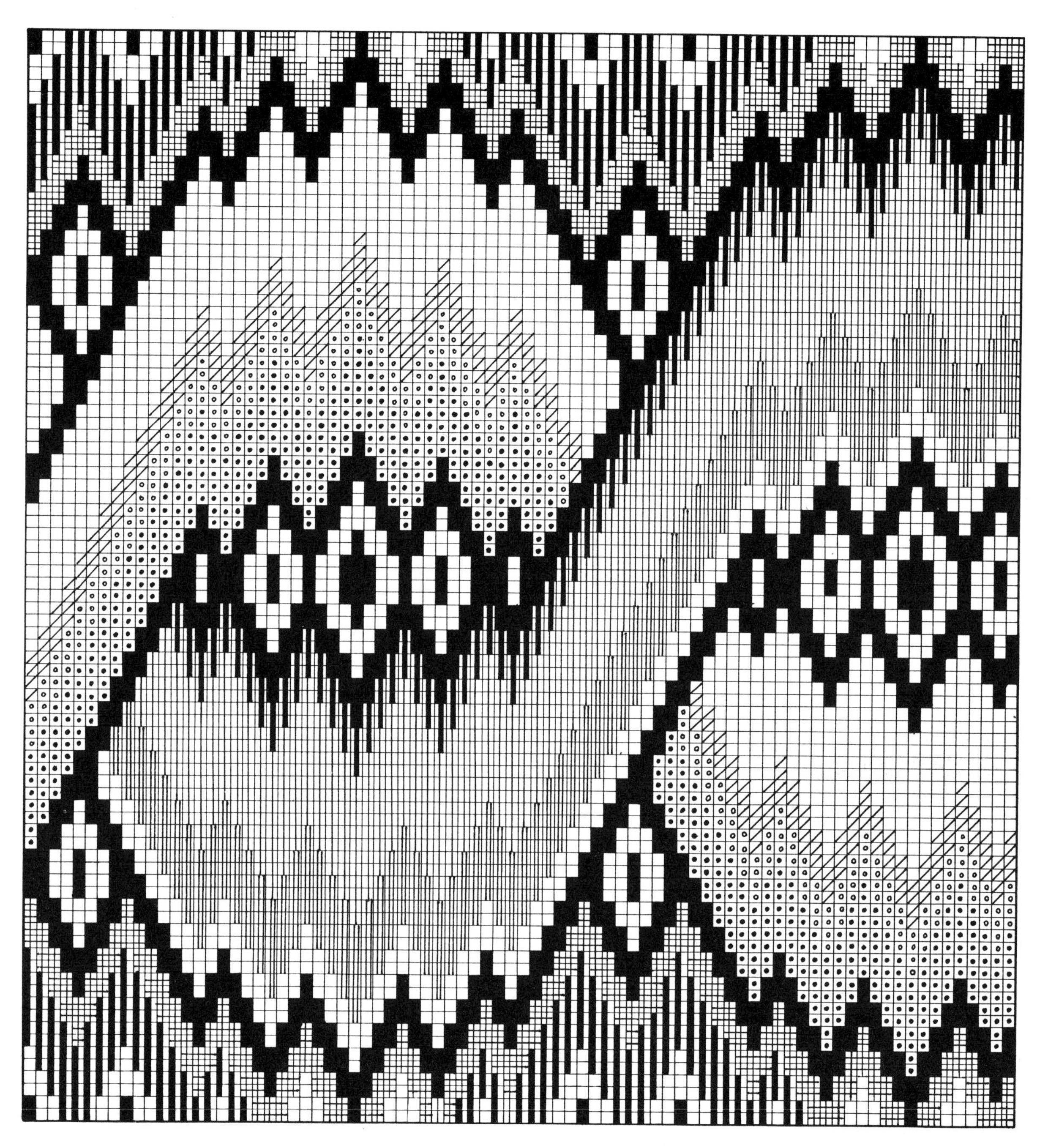

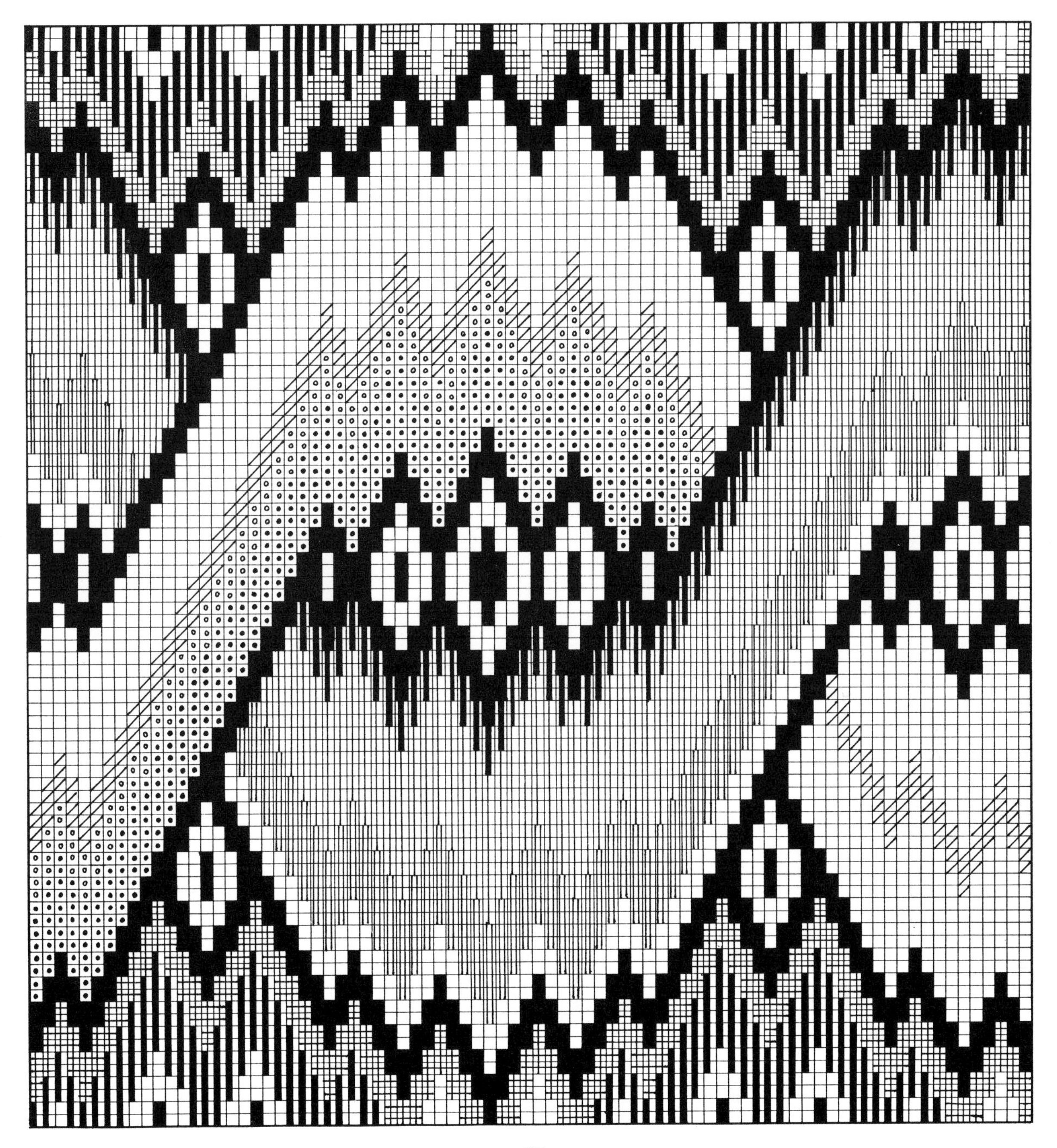

EMBROIDERED HAND-SCREEN

See photograph on facing page
Woollen canvas embroidered with silks in Florentine stitch.
ENGLISH, dated 1718 and initialled 'D.H.' (for Dorcas Haines).
Height (widest) $10\frac{1}{2}$in × $9\frac{3}{4}$in
Pattern repeat (two motifs in width) $3\frac{5}{8}$in × $2\frac{1}{2}$in
Given by Mrs Graham Kerr
Museum no. T.93–1934

Key to chart on pages 50–51

Florentine stitch: 4 squares = 1 stitch

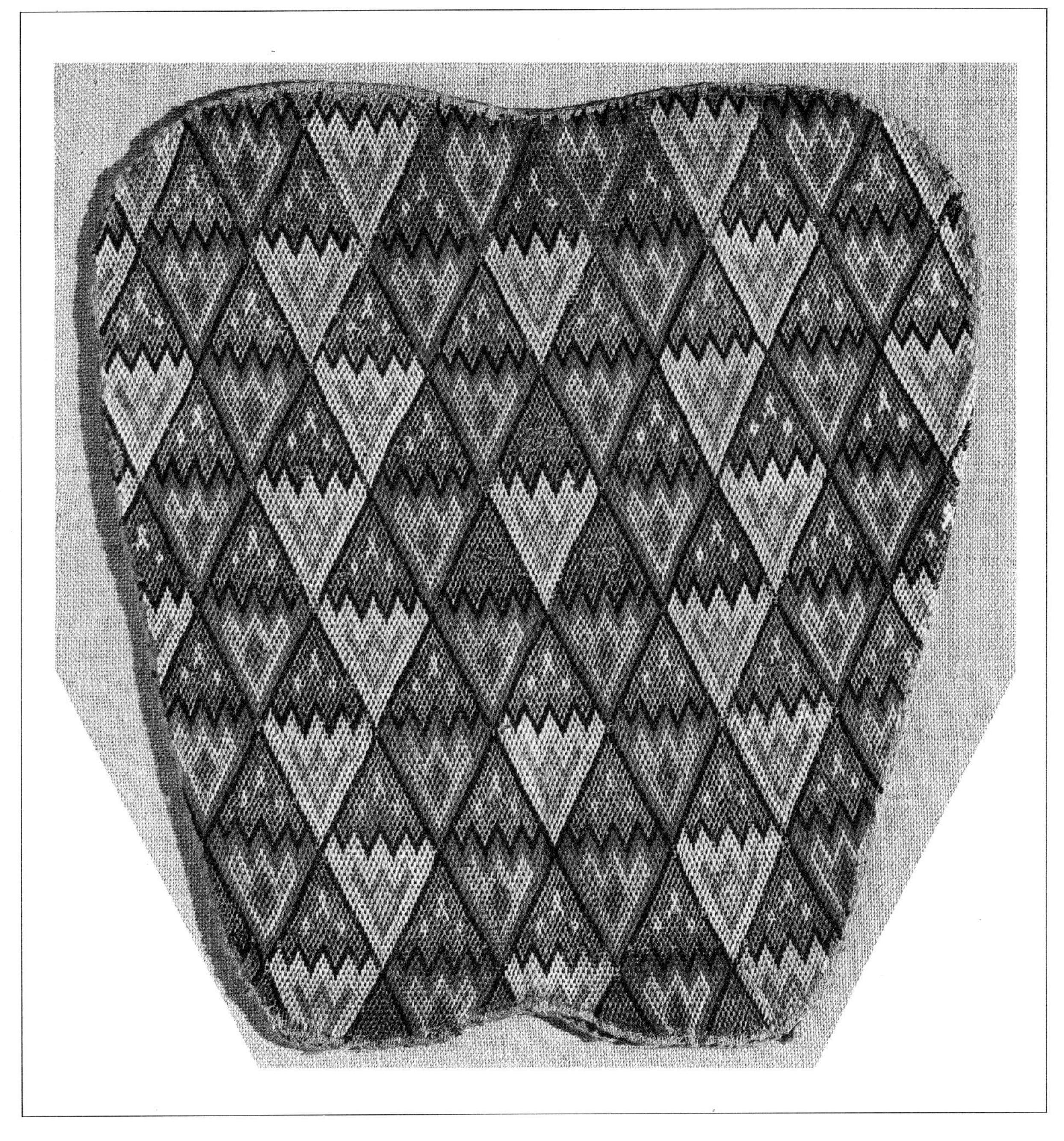

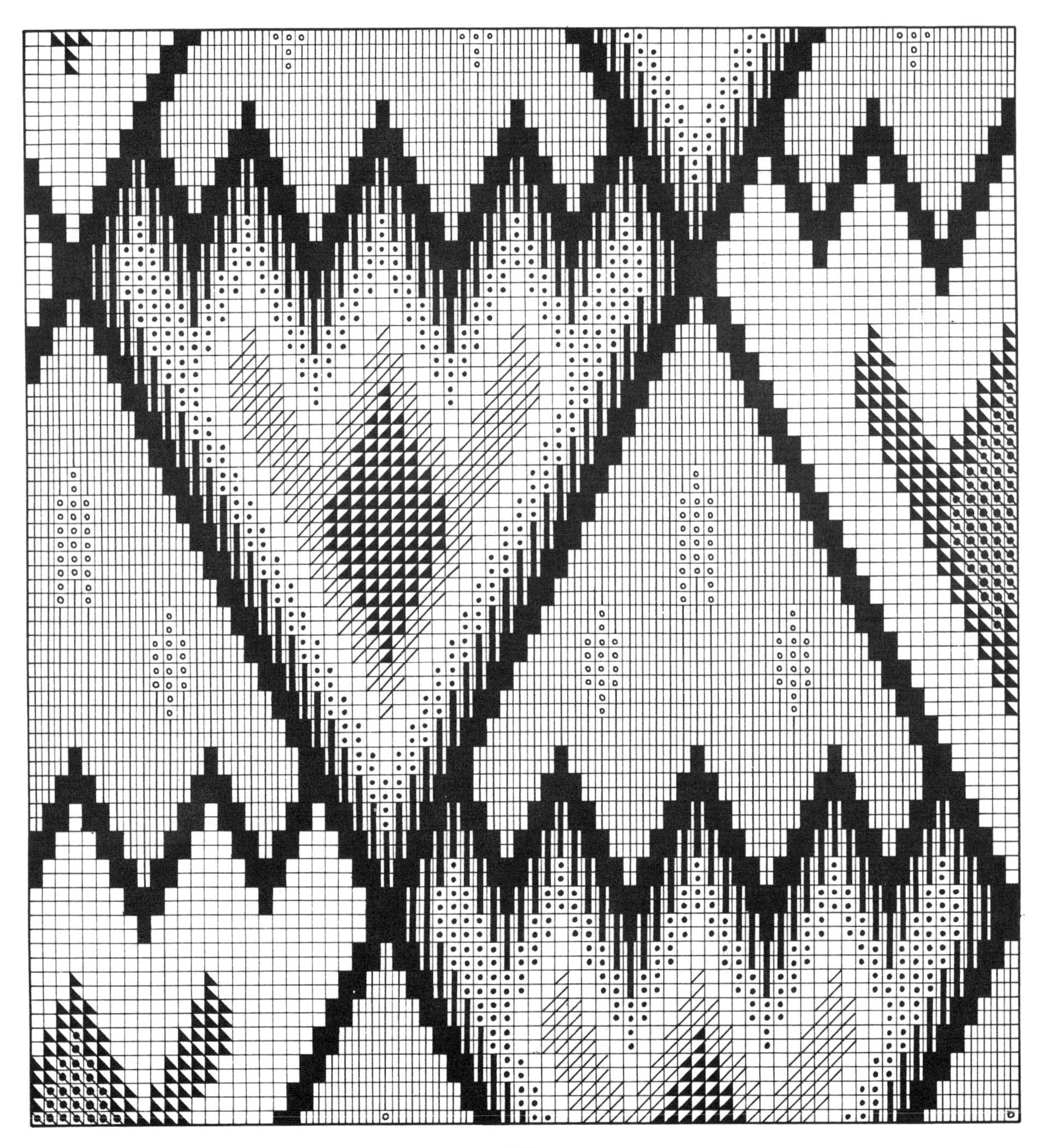

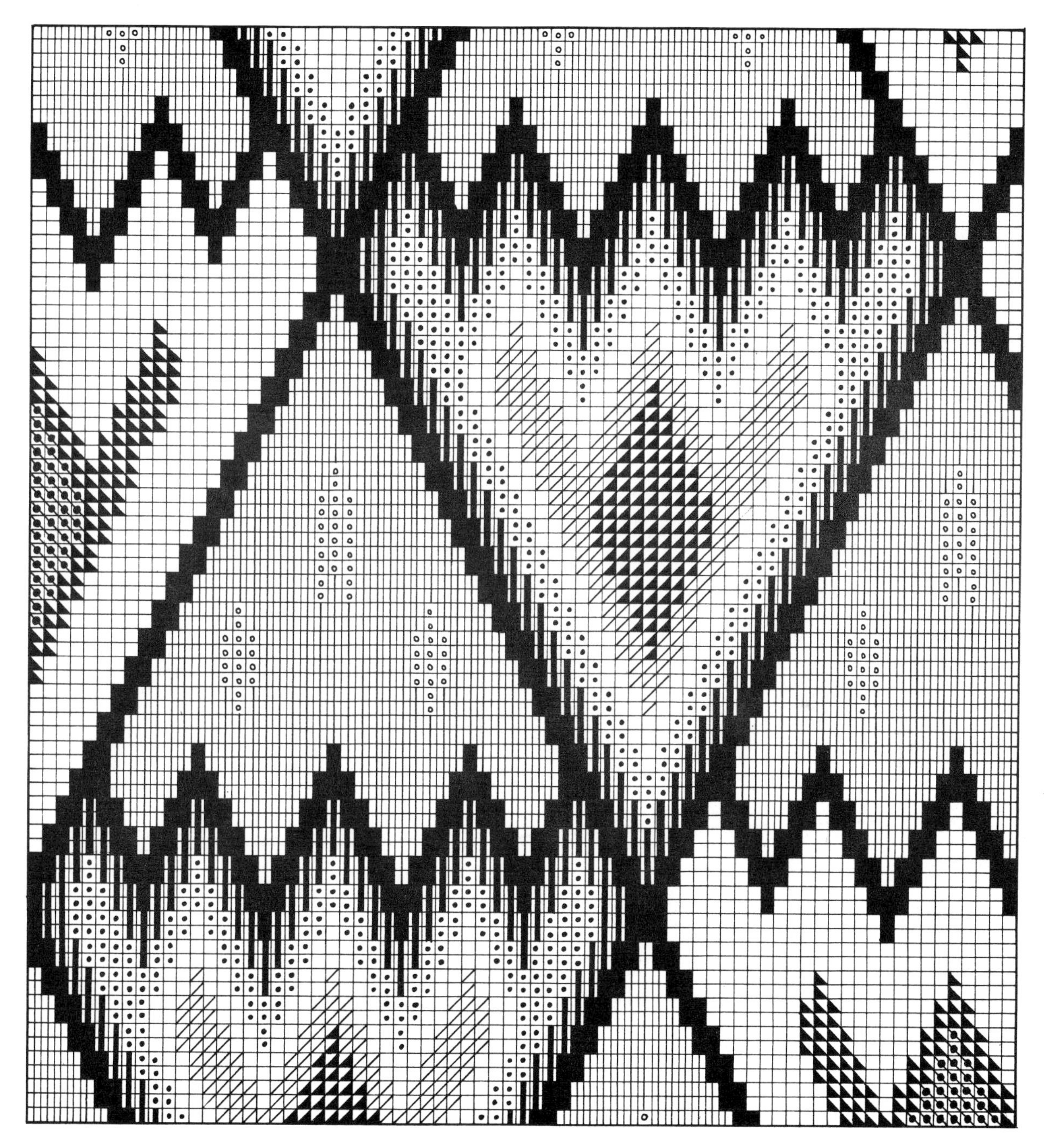

EMBROIDERED CHAIR SEAT PANEL

See photograph on facing page

Closely woven linen canvas embroidered with wools and silks in Florentine stitch. The cream coloured ground and edges to the flowers are embroidered in silks, the remainder in wools.

ENGLISH, second quarter of the 18th century

Height $15\frac{3}{4}$in × $20\frac{3}{4}$in

Pattern repeat: $3\frac{1}{4}$in × $3\frac{7}{8}$in

Given by Mrs E. Low Bright-Williams

Museum no. T.46–1926

Key to charts on pages 54–55

Florentine stitch: 2 squares = 1 stitch

brown

cream

pale pink

pink

dark pink

rust

dark green

yellow/green

mid-green

sea green

very dark green

DETAILS FROM A SET OF BERLIN WOOLWORK SAMPLERS

See photographs on pages 57 and 61

Cotton double canvas (called 'Penelope') embroidered with wools and silks in cross and tent stitch with some metal bead decoration.

ENGLISH, mid-19th century. Embroidered by Miss Sarah Bland (1810–1905)

Each whole canvas sampler strip approx. height $8\frac{1}{2}$in × $53\frac{1}{2}$in

Details charted:

butterfly – Height $1\frac{1}{2}$in × $2\frac{1}{2}$in (worked in tent stitch)
tartan design – Height 2in × $2\frac{1}{4}$in (worked in cross stitch)
ribbon – Height 2in × 3in (worked in cross stitch)
tassels – Height $2\frac{3}{4}$in × 3in (worked in cross stitch)

Given by Mrs D. M. McGregor

Museum nos. T.238, 239, 240–1967

Part of the sampler (the pink butterfly is charted on page 58)

Key to Butterfly chart above (For key to Tartan chart on facing page see page 60)

Tent stitch: 1 square = 1 stitch

■	maroon	pink	◪
◩	crimson	rust	☒
⊟	red	green	⊡

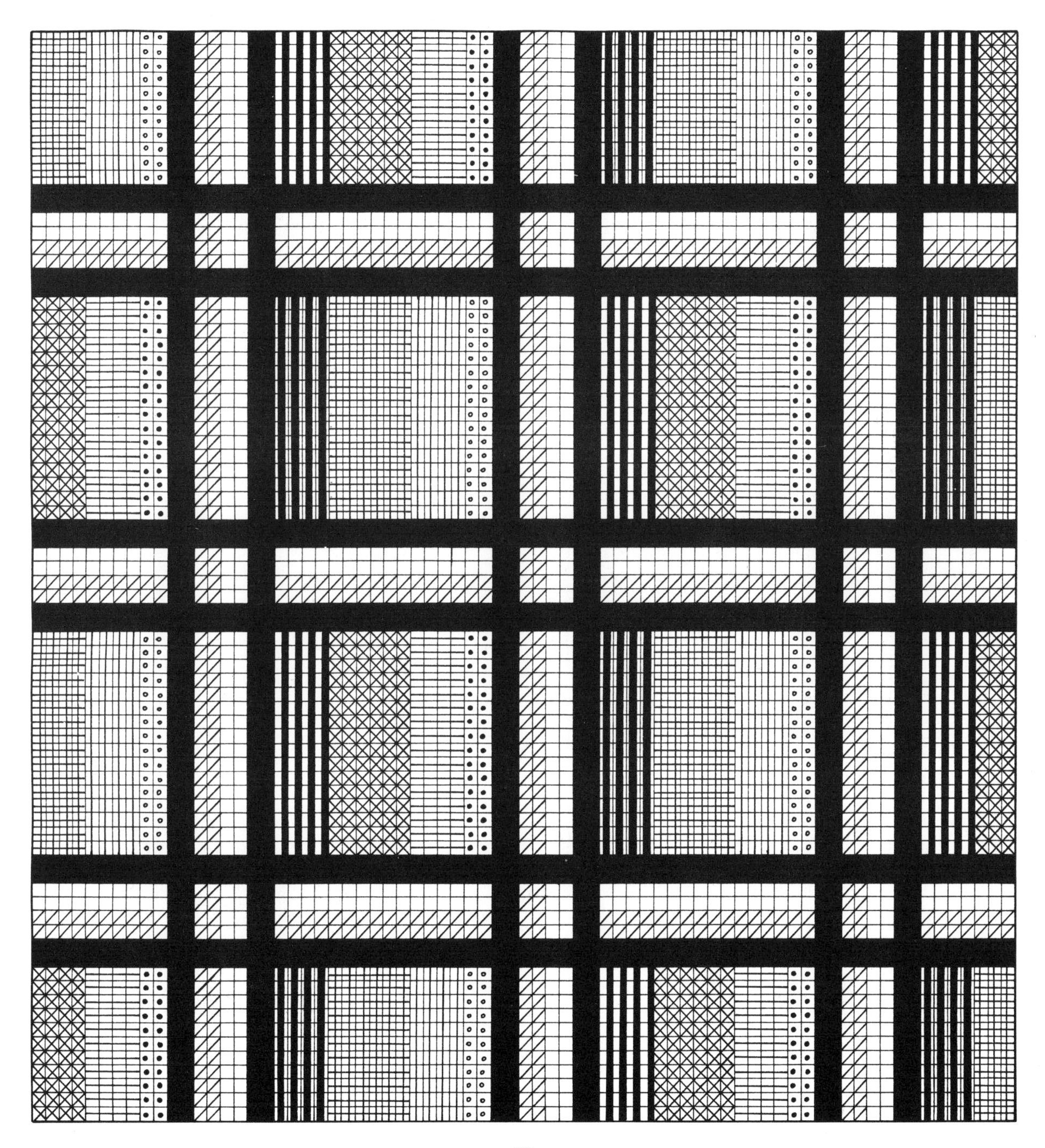

Key to chart on page 59

Cross stitch: 4 squares = 1 stitch

Key to Tassels chart on page 63

Cross stitch: 4 squares = 1 stitch

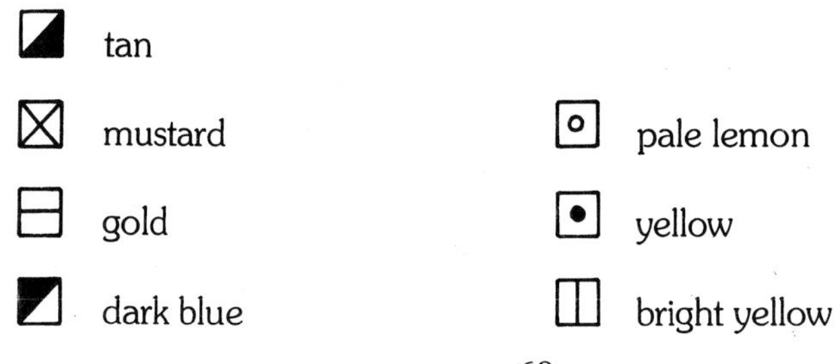

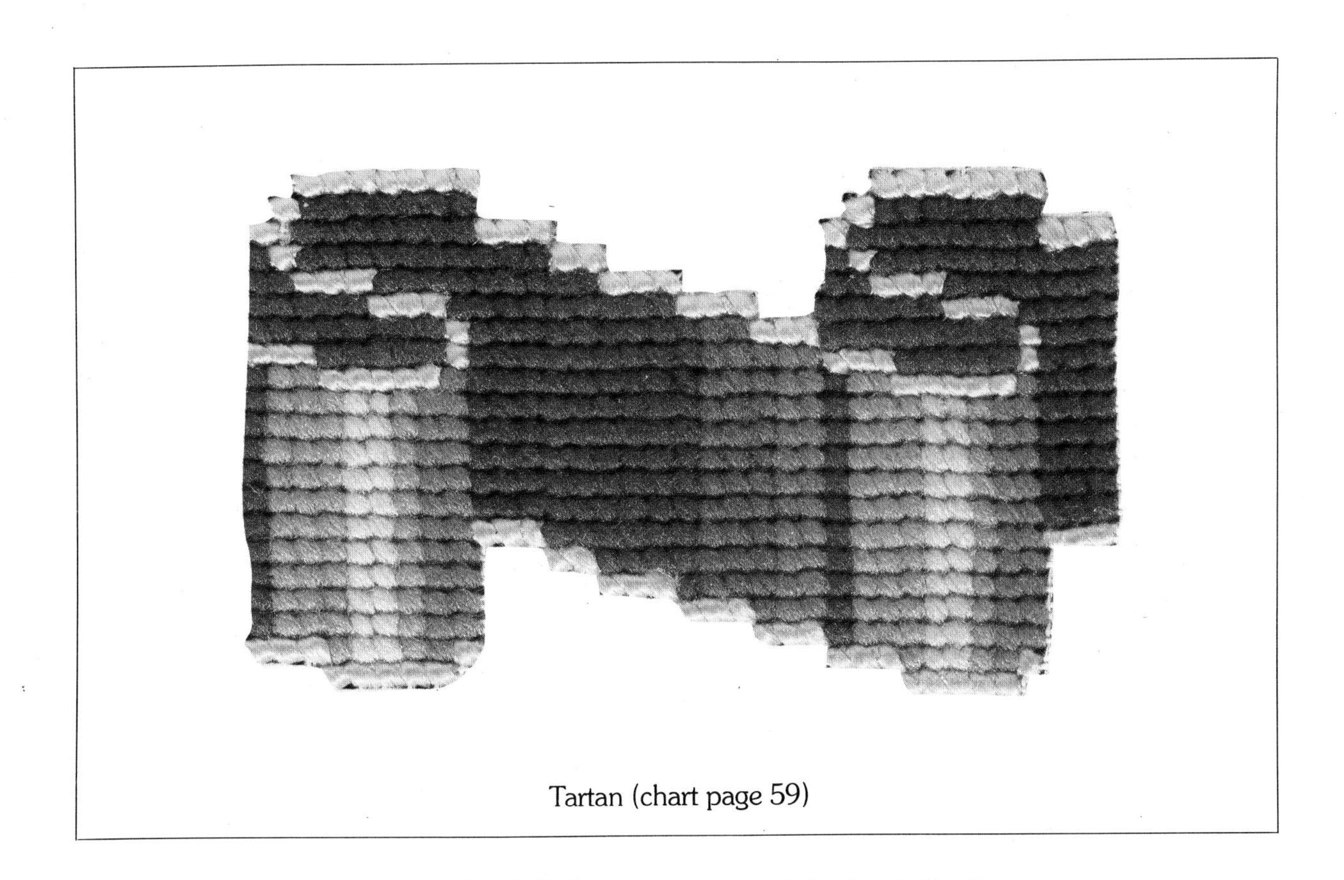

Tartan (chart page 59)

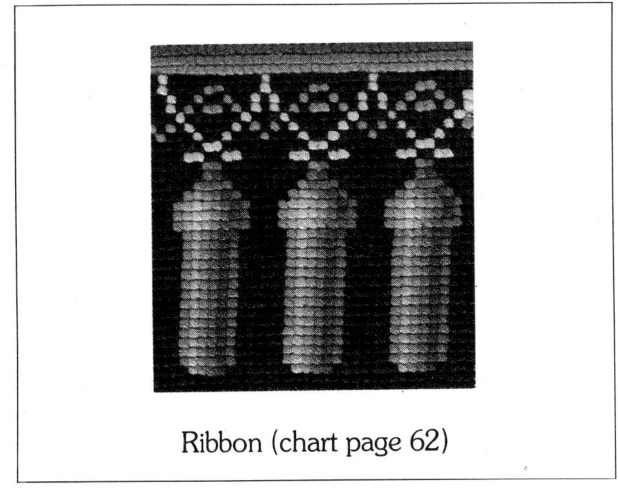

Ribbon (chart page 62)

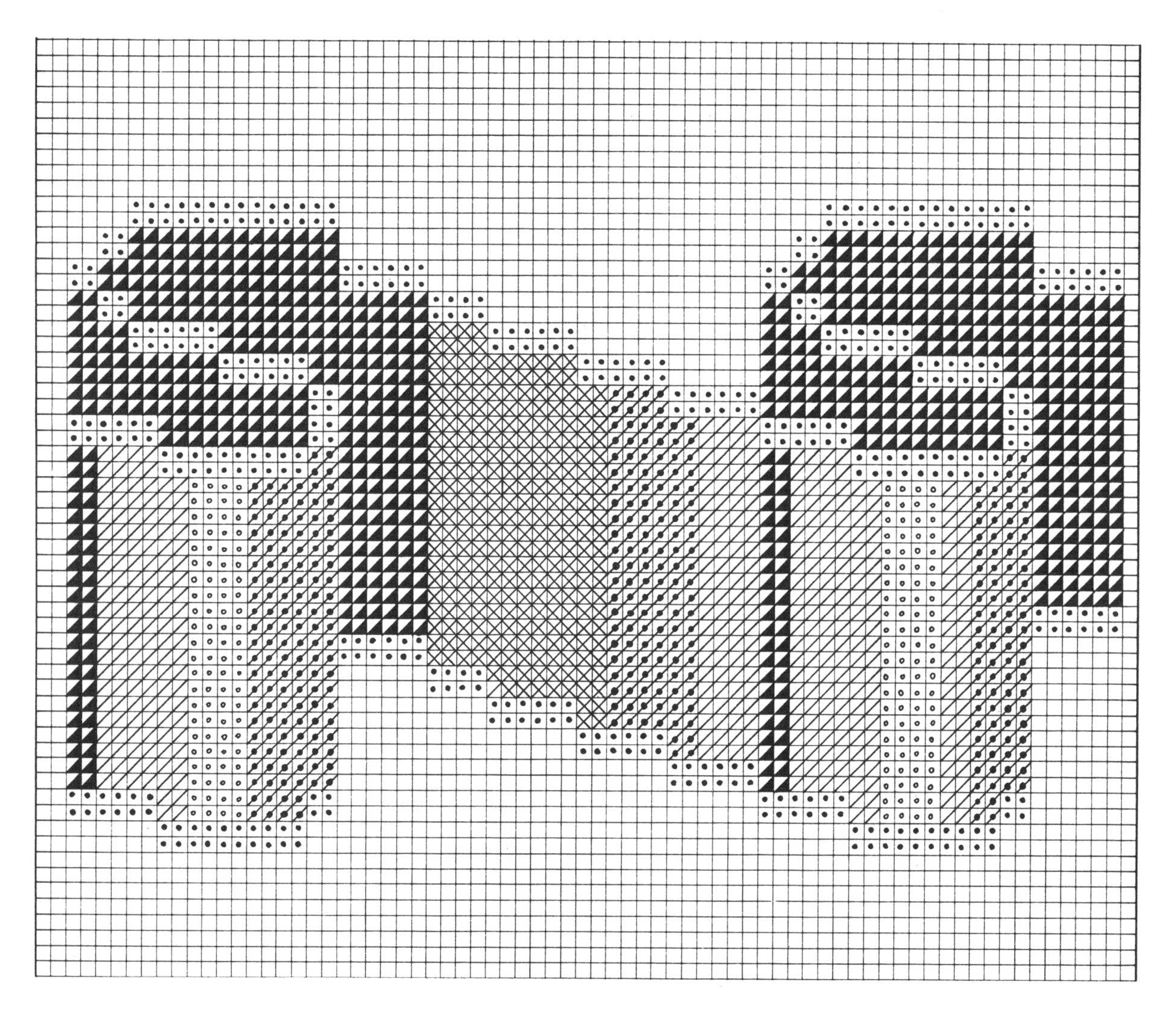

Key to Ribbon chart above (For key to Tassels chart opposite see page 60)
Cross stitch: 4 squares = 1 stitch

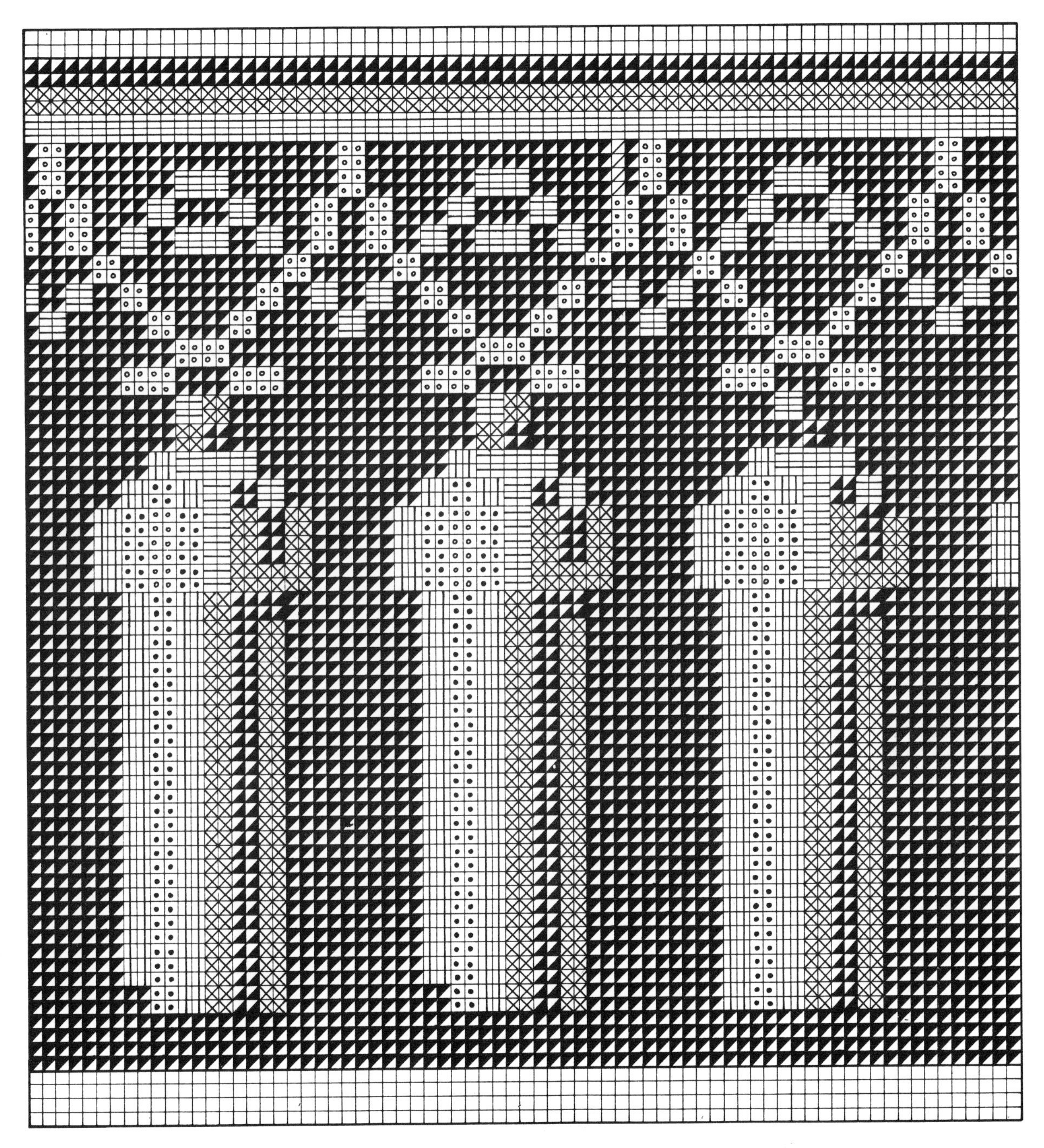

Berlin Woolwork Sampler (see page 66)

FLORAL MOTIF FROM BERLIN WOOLWORK SAMPLER

See photograph on pages 64–65
Cotton 'Penelope' canvas embroidered with wools and silks in cross stitch.
ENGLISH, mid-19th century
Whole bordered design: 5in × 8in
Detail charted $1\frac{1}{2}$in × 2in
Given by Miss E. M. Hall in memory of her sister.
Museum no. T.125B–1956

Key to chart opposite

Cross stitch: 4 squares = 1 stitch

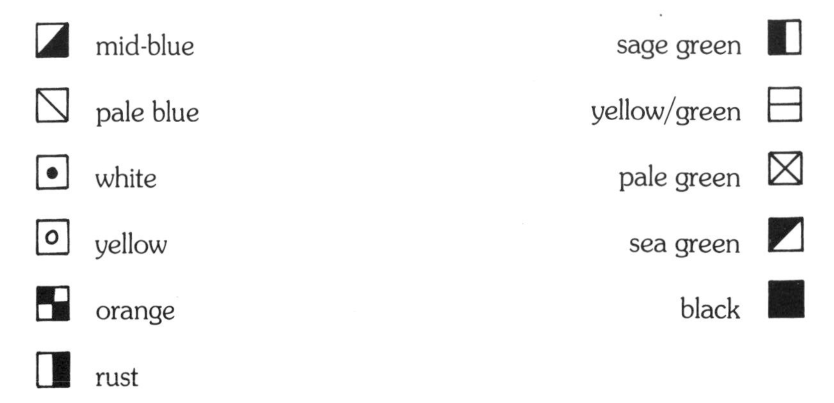

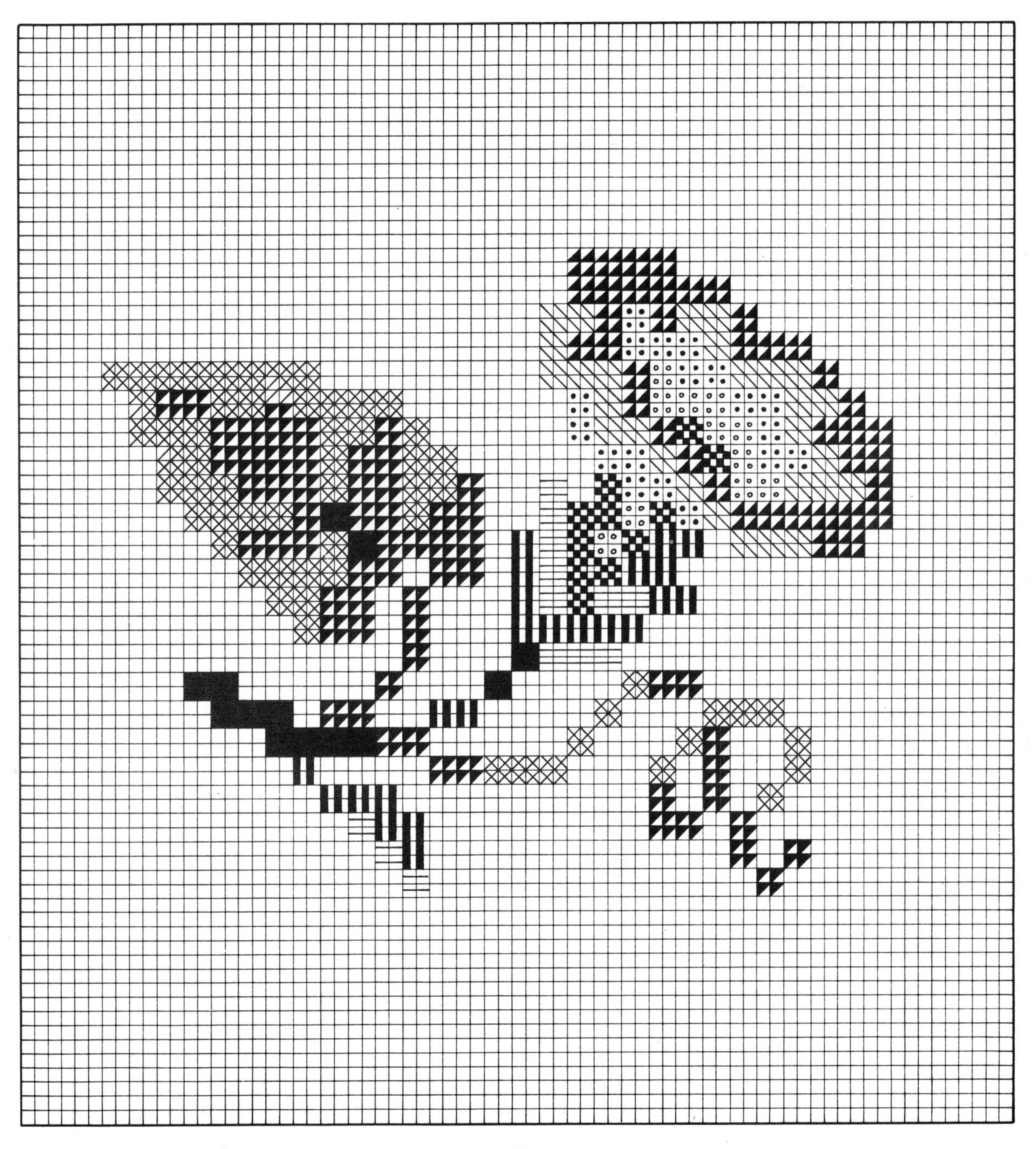

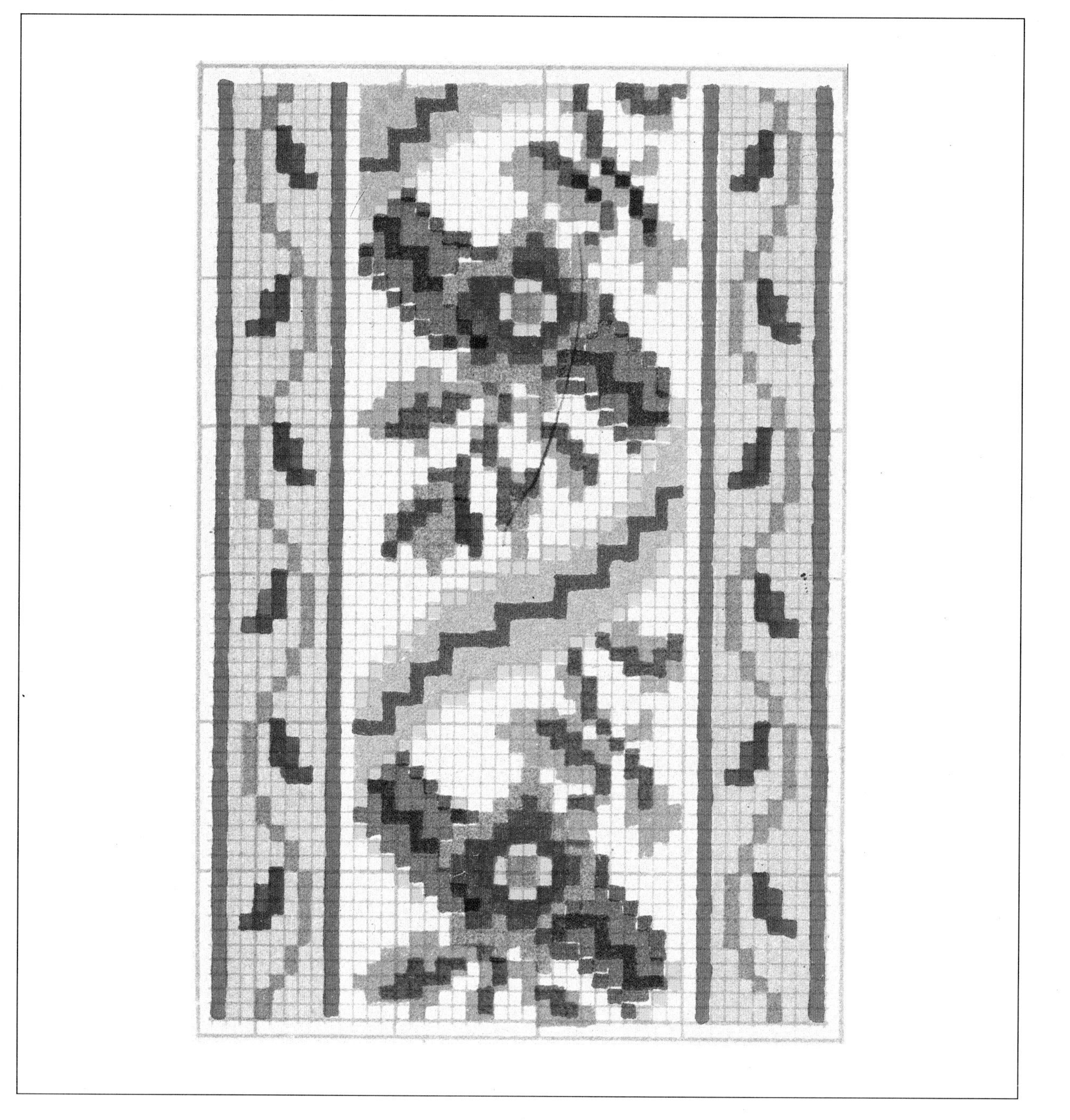

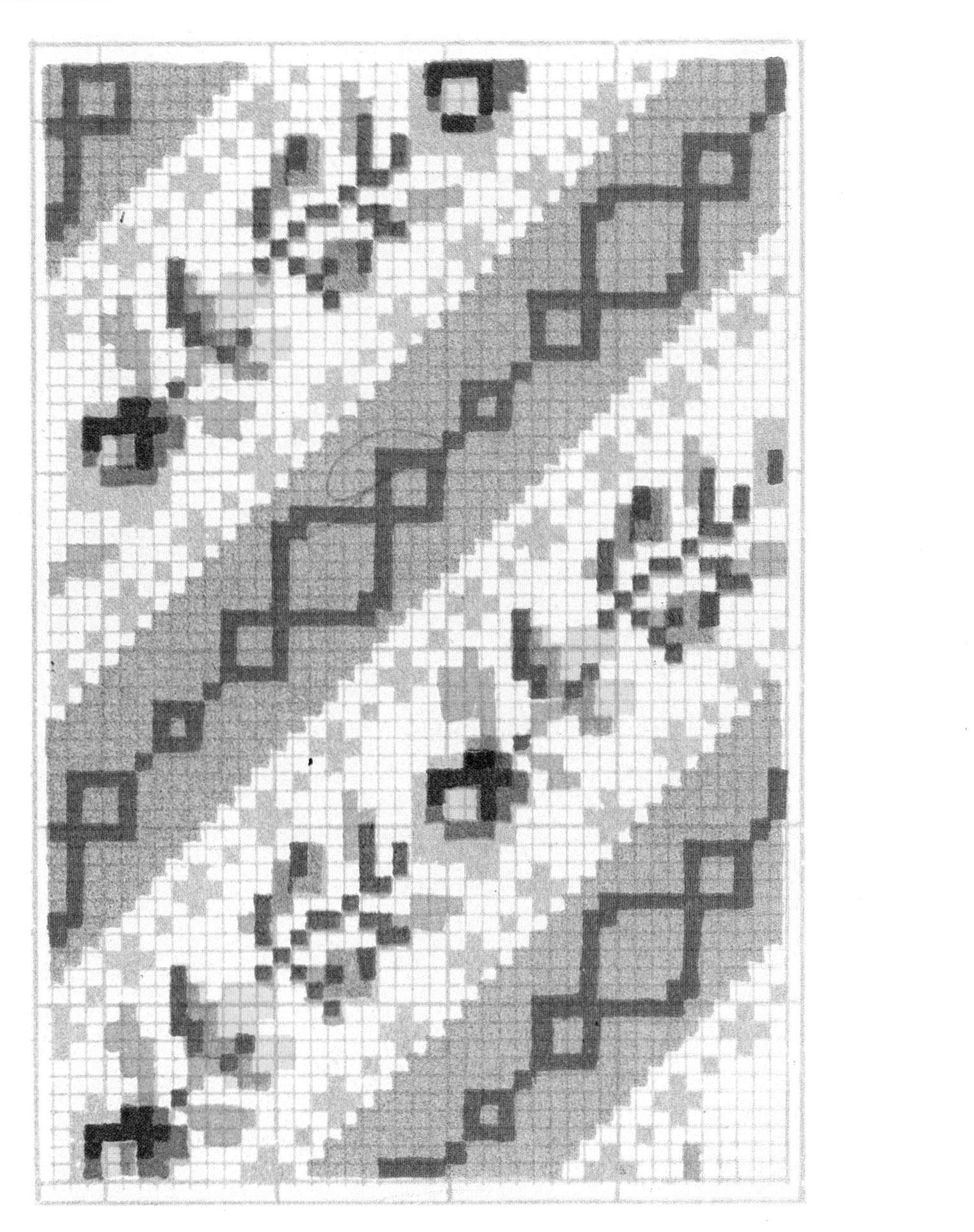

Two pages from a printed pattern book (see page 70)

DESIGNS FROM A PRINTED PATTERN BOOK

See photographs on pages 68–69
Chromolithograph charts from 'Manuel Tapisseries No. 153'.
Intended to be embroidered with silks or wools on any size of canvas.
FRENCH, mid-19th century. Published by N. Alexandre & Cie, Maurice Lajeunesse, Sucr. Editr., Rue St. Martin, Paris.
Page size: $4\frac{1}{2}$in × $6\frac{3}{8}$in

PRINTED BORDER DESIGN

See photograph on page 72

Taken from a manual on cross-stitch embroidery this chromolithograph pattern was published as part of the D.M.C. Library edited by Thérèse de Dillmont.

Intended to be copied in 'cotton, flax and silk threads'

The size of the canvas is not specified and the patterns could also be worked as counted thread embroidery on a closely woven ground.

FRENCH, early 20th century. Published by Dollfus-Mieg & Cie, Société anonyme, Mulhouse-Belfort-Paris.

Detail shown: $5\frac{1}{2}$in × 7in

Printed border designs (see previous page)